THE END OF TIME

By the same author

The miracles of Jesus

JOSEPH RHYMER

THE
END OF TIME

Eschatology of the New Testament

St Paul Publications

The Scripture quotations herein are from the Revised Standard Version of the Bible, Catholic edition, copyright 1965 and 1966 by the Division of Christian Education of the National Council of the Churches of Christ in the USA, and are used by permission. All rights reserved.

Cover by: *The seven angels with the seven plagues.* Miniature. Sec. XIV.
© Edizioni Paoline, Cinisello Balsamo (Mi), Italy

St Paul Publications
Middlegreen, Slough SL3 6BT, United Kingdom
Moyglare Road, Maynooth, Co. Kildare, Ireland

© Joseph Rhymer 1992
ISBN 085439 404 4
Printed by The Guernsey Press Co., Guernsey, C.I.

St Paul Publications is an activity of the priests and brothers of the Society of St Paul who proclaim the Gospel through the media of social communication

Contents

Introduction — 7

Part 1. TIME FULFILLED — 11

1. The cosmic pattern of love and justice — 11
2. The gospels of fulfilment — 21
3. The climax of the Gospels — 35
4. The first Christians and their Letters — 51

Part 2. THE BOOK OF REVELATION — 65

5. Christ's judgement of the Churches (Rev 1:1–3:22) — 65
6. Heaven and the scroll with seven seals (Rev 4:1–8:1) — 79
7. The seven trumpets (Rev 8:2–11:19) — 93
8. The woman, the dragon and the two beasts (Rev 12:1–13:18) — 105
9. The triumph of the Lamb over Babylon (Rev 14:1–20:15) — 115
10. The new creation (Rev 21:1–22:21) — 133

Conclusion — 143

Suggestions for further reading — 151
General Index — 153
Index of Biblical references — 155

Introduction

Many people who do not actually go to church seem to think that Christianity is mainly a religion of doom and gloom, which emphasises that the end of the world will happen at any moment and everyone will immediately have to face a stern God who is swift to condemn people to hell. By contrast, practising members of the larger Christian denominations will know that there is not much mention in today's Churches of beliefs which might give this impression. These may be summarized as the beliefs about 'the final times', and they include such topics as death, the end of the universe, the second coming of Jesus, the resurrection of the dead, the Last Judgement, heaven and hell.

Most main-line Christians – including the clergy – now seem to avoid these areas because they represent the 'darker' aspects of Christian belief. They still feature in official Church statements, such as the documents of the Second Vatican Council, but they have all but vanished from the pulpit and the religious press. Yet the evidence of religious art, poetry and music, shows that until recently these aspects of Christianity featured prominently in popular preaching and teaching.

A browse through the hymn books currently in use in churches reveals that there are still a lot of hymns available which feature these teachings, such as 'Lo! He comes with clouds descending, once for favoured sinners slain;' and even 'O come, O come, Emmanuel, and ransom captive Israel.' But where such hymns are still in use they have either been turned into Christmas carols, or they are only sung during Advent when everyone's mind is on Christmas. Consequently, the 'coming' of Jesus is unthinkingly referred to his nativity rather than to his second coming in judgement.

Until the end of the 1960's Catholics were reminded of the Church's stark teachings about the Last Judgement on All Souls' Day, 2nd November, and whenever they went to a Requiem Mass at a funeral. They were reminded because the order of service contained the long thirteenth century hymn 'Dies Irae'.

'Day of wrath and terror looming,
Heaven and earth to ash consuming,
Seer's and Psalmist's true foreboding.

Ah, what agony of trembling,
When the Judge, mankind assembling,
Probeth all beyond dissembling...'

By 1970 this had disappeared as a required part of such services, and it could no longer be found in the missals authorized for popular use. The 'Dies Irae' still remains an option, and the ordinary worshipper may still find it used by the priest immediately after the death of someone, at the vigil service when the body is received into the church, at the Requiem Mass and at the burial or cremation; but it has to be said that this is increasingly unlikely.

The emphasis at times associated with death has moved strongly towards sharing in the resurrection of Jesus rather than facing him in judgement, and this is admirable. But the change may also be part of the general tendency in our society to refuse to face the full reality of personal moral responsibility and of death.

There are still times, however, when we are stopped in our tracks by the frailty of human life and its institutions. One such time is the death of a close relative or friend, especially if it is sudden death in our presence. Another is the experience of whole cities or countries being destroyed or devastated by war. Yet another is the recurrence of genocide, the systematic attempt to exterminate whole social or ethnic groups by the million, which has been practised on an unprecedented scale within our own times. And there is the growing concern about ecological damage to the whole world environment, which became a conscious public issue with the use of nuclear power as a weapon of war. Any one of these, let alone all of them, can force people to ask the kind of religious questions which invite answers in terms of the world's 'end times', and the kind of final justice which can only come from God.

Even in the most prosperous regions of the ancient world, people lived in the very midst of sudden death from sickness or famine. There was also the constant danger of communal violence and warfare which could eliminate whole communities or banish them into slavery. And natural disasters brought home to all the fragility of the physical world. These experiences engendered and nurtured the ancient religious beliefs about the end of the world, divine judgement, and reward or punishment beyond this life.

Christianity inherited such older beliefs, especially those expressed in the Hebrew sacred writings, the 'Old Testament', along with all their vivid language. But Christianity added a unique dimension to such beliefs and reshaped them by relating them to the teachings of Jesus and to his death, resurrection and ascension. It transformed them by relating them all to the new understanding of the love of God revealed and made available to all by Jesus Christ.

This book is an exposition of the sources of the traditional Christian beliefs and language about 'the end times', whether they are the end for the individual's life on earth, the end for whole communities, or even the end of the whole universe. All too often in the history of Christianity these beliefs have been used to strike fear into people's hearts, to frighten them into trying to draw closer to God or to coerce them into obedience of rulers for less worthy motives.

Despite the ways that Christian beliefs have often been presented and misused, the essential Christian message has been one of reassurance right from its earliest times: that there are no grounds for fear when people really accept that God is love and that he shares his love with them freely and completely:

'God is love, and whoever lives in love lives in union with God, and God is in union with him. Love is perfected in us, so that we may face the Day of Judgement without fear; we can do this because our life in this world is already the same as Christ's. There is no fear in love, for perfect love casts out all fear' (1 Jn 4:16-18).

As we shall see, Christian beliefs about 'the final times' should be related to the wider context of God's love, then there is no need to push them into the background. They are an essential part of the 'good news' revealed by Jesus Christ, and the Christian message of hope is weakened if they are ignored.

Part 1:
TIME FULFILLED

1

The cosmic pattern of love and justice

The strangest book in the Bible comes at the very end of it, variously known as 'The Book of Revelation', 'The Revelation to John', and 'The Apocalypse' – which is the English form of the Greek word with which the book begins. A strange work it may be, but its words have been the centre of popular attention again and again since it was written, nearly two thousand years ago. It has received special attention towards the end of each century, when people have thought that great changes, perhaps great disasters, were about to occur. This is because the book claims to reveal the details of what is going to happen at the end of the world.

The Bible begins with a description of the creation of the universe and everything in it, including humanity. Those opening eleven chapters of the Book of Genesis could be renamed the Book of Creation. At the other end of the Bible the Book of Revelation describes how the universe will end. Between these two events lies the whole of human history, and the two events combined provide a key to everything that happens in history, both in the past and in the future.

The Book of Creation

The Book of Creation, Genesis 1-11, is a vision of an ideal universe marred by mankind's disobedience. Inspired by God, the original Hebrew authors or editors wove their account of the origins of the universe. They used well known stories about the origins of the world which can also be found in the traditions of many other peoples of the ancient Middle East. But the Hebrews transformed those stories into a wonderful revelation of the true character of God. In other peoples' traditions the gods created the universe, of course, and there are gardens and trees and serpents and great floods. But in these other traditions the gods are at war with each other, and the inhabitants of the world are innocent victims of the resulting carnage, like refugees fleeing before an invasion, or peasants caught up in the savage feuds of an aristocracy.

For the Hebrews, the God of creation in the Book of Genesis is the only God and the source of all goodness. The whole creation forms a single, ordered universe where everything has its proper place and can find its fulfilment without harm to anything else. Mankind – both men and women – is appointed by God to administer it all according to God's master plan, like wise ministers of a wise king.

But like a modern reader, the ancient Hebrews were all too aware that the world in which they lived did not seem like that. It is experienced as a flawed creation, corrupt and threatening, where the weak and innocent are at the mercy of the strong. The creation stories lay the blame for this corruption firmly on the shoulders of mankind. They depict a God who from the beginning has given people freedom, so that they could respond to him in love, not fear. They have the personal dignity of responsible adults, not the subservience of slaves who only obey because they are forced to do so. The Fall depicts – in story form – mankind as Adam and Eve, misusing their freedom and seeking power over the creation in their own right, independently of God. They obtained the power they sought, for God would not destroy their freedom, but he limited their capacity to do harm by banishing them from the garden at the centre of the universe.

The story of the flood is also found in other traditions, but the Hebrews turned it into an assertion of God's sovereign authority as judge. Mankind created disorder, but God could not allow it to triumph, so God unleashed destruction on his creation to be rid of the evil. But a thread of mercy is woven into the tapestry of cosmic punishment; a righteous man – Noah – and his family ride out the storm in the boat God ordered them to build, together with all the animal stock for a new beginning.

The story of the flood shows God eliminating the fruits of disorder and evil, but the causes themselves cannot be destroyed because they are rooted in mankind's abuse of its freedom. Nevertheless, the evil tendencies in mankind might be controlled by wise laws if people would only accept them. So God reveals laws to a chosen people, the Hebrews, selected by him to respond with loving obedience. As it unfolds, the story makes it clear that God chose the Hebrews to be a living example to the rest of the world; they were to be a chosen people who would eventually attract all peoples back to God again.

The opening chapters of Genesis, 'The Book of Creation', are placed there as an introduction and explanation of all that follows. The rest of the Bible draws a stark contrast between the harsh reality of the world's history and God's wishes for all the peoples of his creation. God has not abdicated his sovereign powers, but he will do nothing which destroys his people's responsibility, their power to respond. They must recognise that God is love, and relate to him in free and loving response; by definition, he cannot force them to do that.

The Messiah, saviour and judge

The pattern of God's love is revealed in the Old Testament, but it is only revealed slowly, like a great carpet which shows more and more of the Master Weaver's design as it emerges from an immense loom. Christians believe that the pattern was completed by the birth, life, death, resurrection and ascension of Jesus Christ – Jesus the Messiah.

For Christians, the most important revelations in the Old Testament are about the Messiah and the coming reign of God. This hope in the Messiah and the Messianic Age is expressed in a whole range of images and ideas which carry the experience gained by past generations of Hebrews as they wrestled with God's choice of their nation and asked how he had shown his presence to them in their history. These beliefs point to the future rather than the past; they express belief in a messianic future far more wonderful than anything their ancestors experienced, yet it is a future which makes sense of the past.

More important still, their beliefs about the Messiah made it possible for the Hebrew people to bear with their present circumstances when it appeared that God had deserted them. They could fit their sufferings and humiliations into a broader pattern of confident belief, which reassured them that they were still the people God had chosen.

They looked forward to a time when the presence of God would be recognised and acknowledged by all, Jew and Gentile alike. The whole world would be ruled by an ideal king, the nation would be prosperous and all peoples would look to Jerusalem for its salvation. It would be a time for rewards and glory, but it would also bring justice and punishment for all who refused to acknowledge God's rule or who persecuted his people. When that time came God's will would prevail and no power in the universe would be able to oppose it.

A wide range of vivid images and folk memories were available from the nation's history to express the deep feelings and longings embodied in the idea of the Messiah. The most powerful of these was the exodus – the escape from Egypt – and the covenant at Mount Sinai so closely associated with it (Ex 14:19-24). The memory of King David also had a strong hold on the people's imagination because of the brief period of national independence and prosperity under the rule of David and his son, King Solomon. David came to the Hebrew throne about 200 years after the exodus. He gave his people their first secure hold on the land of Palestine, and he and

Solomon united the warring Hebrew tribes around the new national capital, Jerusalem, and its new temple.

Soon afterwards, the prophets began to say that God's patience and faithfulness towards his chosen people was like the love between husband and wife in a good marriage. Even though the people failed God and deserted him, they were his bride and he was always ready to receive them back and forgive them.

Subsequent Hebrew kings and their officials failed to rule by the standards of the divine covenant. The prophets condemned them and promised that God would not leave his people at their mercy. He would send them a good shepherd who would arrive miraculously from heaven, overthrow all the people's enemies and establish God's just rule on earth. There would be a new covenant which would transform the people's hearts, and it would reach out from the Hebrews to all the nations of the earth. There is just a hint that the rule of God might only be achieved after God's shepherd-servant has been rejected, maltreated and killed.

There are also dark and violent images of war, retribution and suffering, of glorious rewards and terrible punishments, when God finally administers justice to his creation. These Old Testament prophecies of the final times are sometimes called 'apocalyptic', because their imagery comes to its climax in 'The Apocalypse', the last book of the New Testament. But they permeate the other books of the New Testament as well: the four Gospels, the Acts of the Apostles and the Letters. The whole of the New Testament was written by Christians who believed that they were living at the end of time itself. Looking back into these complex experiences and hopes of the people of the Old Testament, the first Christians saw them all pointing forward towards Jesus, the Messiah who fulfilled everything that God had ever promised.

The Gospels

For Christians, all the hopes centred on the Messiah and the whole drama of God's love reach their climax with the birth of Jesus Christ, who is love incarnate and the fullest possible revelation of God to the human race. Jesus reveals in his own life the infinite depths and indestructible power of God's love. He reveals it in everything he does and says, but he reveals it most vividly by dying and rising again, and by making his life available to all who want to love God. At the stage in history reached in the Gospels, God does not eliminate the evil disorder in his universe, but he shows in Christ that evil has no real power over those who respond freely to God in unconditional love.

The Gospels are about Jesus Christ: his birth, ministry, rejection and crucifixion; his resurrection and ascension. But they present all this as the beginning of the final stage of history when God will overcome all evil in the universe and bring the whole creation to the state of perfection he had always planned for it.

Behind the four Gospels there lies the testimony of the inner circle of people close to Jesus, particularly the disciple-apostles whom Jesus chose to be with him during his public ministry. These apostles obeyed his command to teach the world about Jesus after his death, resurrection and ascension, and the New Testament records the outlines of their addresses and sermons. These records show that the apostles made six main points about Jesus in their message of 'good news' to the world:

1. Jesus is the saviour promised in the Jewish sacred writings, the books of the Old Testament, which the first Christians accepted as God's revelation;

2. Jesus inaugurated this new era of salvation for the whole world by means of his birth, ministry, death and resurrection from the dead;

3. Jesus has ascended to heaven, where he now reigns in the name of God as Lord over the whole universe;

4. Jesus has sent the Holy Spirit as proof of his power so that all who believe in him may share in his salvation;

5. Jesus will come again as judge, to bring all history to a close and to complete God's plans for a new universe;

6. Anyone in the world can share in the salvation Jesus has achieved – and can receive the Holy Spirit – by repenting, believing and being baptised.

The four Gospels were written around this pattern of teaching; if anyone reads the Gospels without recognising this, the Gospel stories will lose most of their point however moving they may be. All the information which the Gospels provide about Jesus has been selected and arranged to illustrate this pattern of beliefs about him. And the beliefs about the second coming of Jesus are just as important as the rest.

Paul, the first Christians and the Apocalypse

Not surprisingly, a similar pattern of Christian beliefs lies behind the collection of Letters contained in the New Testament, most of which were written by St Paul to the Churches he founded during his missionary journeys. His readers knew these beliefs well, for like Paul himself they too had learned summaries of belief about Jesus during their period of instruction, so that they could repeat them as acts of faith when they were baptised and received as Christians. One of the briefest examples is given by Paul in his Letter to the Romans:

> '...if you declare with your mouth that Jesus is Lord, and if you believe with your heart that God raised him from the dead, then you will be saved' (Rom 10:9).

A far more extensive example occurs in Paul's Letter to the Colossians, where Paul quotes one of the hymns Christians sang when they gathered for worship:

> 'He is the image of the unseen God, the first-born of all creation,
> for in him were created all things in heaven and on earth: everything visible and everything invisible,

thrones, ruling forces, sovereignties, powers –
all things were created through him and for him.
He exists before all things and in him all things hold together,
and he is the Head of the Body, that is, the Church.

He is the beginning, the first-born from the dead,
so that he should be supreme in every way;
because God wanted all fullness to be found in him,
and through him to reconcile all things to him,
everything in heaven and everything on earth,
by making peace through his death on the
    cross' (Col 1:15-20).

Such quotations show who Jesus really is, and what he can do for those who believe in him and trust in his saving love. Every story and incident in the four Gospels is an illustration of what these beliefs mean, and of their practical consequences for believers. Every comment and piece of advice in the Letters of the New Testament reinforces these beliefs and applies them to ordinary life.

The first Christians also made sense of the Gospel stories about Jesus by relating them to their own baptism and to their worship of God in the 'breaking of bread' – the Eucharist. In both of these religious rites they believed that they were united with the risen Jesus in all his power; the Gospels helped them to understand what this union meant for them in their everyday lives.

They met as communities for worship, and recognised that they were united with each other by the union they had with the risen and ascended Jesus. But they lived out their lives immersed in the secular world of their own time and place, not withdrawn from it, and they confirmed their beliefs about Jesus in the process of applying them to their everyday experiences. This practical verification of the early beliefs about Jesus is implicit throughout the four Gospels and all the other materials contained in the New Testament, and is central to their credibility.

They knew that Jesus had died and risen from the dead for their generation, all generations and for all creation. Now they eagerly awaited his second coming to complete the whole history of salvation and demonstrate God's final triumph over all evil.

The full, extended description of that final triumph of good over evil and of order over disorder is saved for the last book of the New Testament – the Apocalypse or The Revelation to John – which is a series of visions of the restoration of order and God's rule. In the final battles, the cosmic cataclysm, the judgement and the eternal peace of the kingdom of God, God irresistibly reasserts his rule over the universe.

The traditional Christian beliefs about the Second Coming of Jesus and the end of the world seem no longer to be as prominent as they once were in the larger Christian Churches. This fact explains to some extent why these beliefs are given great prominence by some of the smaller, less conventional or fundamentalist religious organisations who take the Bible more literally than the main Churches. Such beliefs only seem to receive much mention in the Church at seasons such as Advent, the period immediately before Christmas.

Christian art, such as Michelangelo's huge fresco 'The Last Judgement' in the Vatican's Sistine Chapel or Dürer's famous series of woodcuts of the Apocalypse, shows that this neglect of some of Christianity's central beliefs is a recent development. Perhaps the problem lies with the language traditionally used to express these beliefs, which can be horrific. In that case language must be found which conveys the truths of these beliefs to a modern audience, for the Christian truths about judgement and the final destiny of history are far too important to be neglected. They are an essential part of the 'good news' of salvation revealed by Jesus Christ himself.

2
The gospel of fulfilment

At first sight the four Gospels may appear to be simple accounts of the birth, ministry and final days of Jesus Christ, but they are far more subtle than mere biographies. As we have seen, they reflect the pattern of beliefs about Jesus which the first two generations of Christians received when the apostles of Jesus preached to them. These beliefs were reinforced by such Christian rites and acts of worship as baptism and the Eucharist (variously referred to as the Lord's Supper and, subsequently, the Mass).

Christian beliefs about the Messianic Age, the Last Judgement and the future history of God's eternal kingdom receive explicit treatment in the 'eschatological' discourses where Jesus concentrates his teaching on 'the final times' (Mt 24:3-24:46; Mk 13:3-37; Lk 21:7-36. 'Eschatology' comes from the Greek word for 'last'); but these beliefs also permeate all the contents of the Gospels, not just the passages explicitly devoted to them.

The opening claims

Each of the four Gospels has its own way of presenting Jesus. A useful clue to how each Gospel goes about this may be found in the way the first three of the Gospels report what

Jesus first said when he started to preach to the general public:

Mark

'The time is fulfilled, and the kingdom of God is close at hand; repent, and believe in the gospel' (Mk 1:15).

Matthew

'Blessed are the poor in spirit, for theirs is the kingdom of heaven...
Blessed are the meek, for they shall inherit the earth...
Blessed are those who are persecuted for righteousness' sake, for theirs is the kingdom of heaven' (Mt 5:3-10).

Luke

'The Spirit of the Lord is upon me, because he has anointed me to preach good news to the poor.
He has sent me to proclaim release to the captives, and recovering of sight to the blind,
to set at liberty those who are oppressed,
to proclaim the acceptable year of the Lord' (Lk 4:18f).

Each one of these summaries indicates that Jesus told the people that the times of the Messiah had arrived, the climax of the world's history promised in so many different ways by the Old Testament. The times had now been fulfilled, he said, and those now living must hurry to repent and to believe in the good news that the Messiah had come. The long awaited 'kingdom of God' was being proclaimed. The people in the synagogue listening to Jesus in Luke's account had no doubt at all that he was claiming to be the Messiah, and they were so shocked that they tried to kill him for blaspheming.

John

John's Gospel presents Jesus in his cosmic setting; he is the Word of creation. Once John has established that, everything that Jesus did or said and everything that happened to him during his life on earth makes a different kind of sense. 'Word' in English translates 'logos' in the Greek of John's Gospel. It is the basis of our word 'logic', meaning a pattern that reason can grasp and use to explain what is happening.

The endless changes of world history are not just haphazard, says John; there is a stable pattern – a logic – in all the changes; they are part of a single plan of development. This 'logic', says John, was revealed by Jesus at every moment in the pattern of his life, and it opens the mind of God to every human being.

This is one of the strands of thought which helps us to understand what John meant when he referred to Jesus as 'the Word of God'. It means that Jesus embodies God's logic, the pattern that can be seen – once we get the clue to it – in all the creative work of God, past, present and future. The future revealed by Jesus changes all our understanding of the present and the past; in Jesus we now know, says John, what it was all leading up to and where it is really going.

Two other strands in John's thought come from the Old Testament. First, in the opening account of the creation of the world, in Genesis 1, God creates just by word of command, and brings into existence a logical, ordered universe with mankind at its centre. Mankind is made in God's own image, to understand the logic of the universe and to administer it in communion with God and in accordance with God's logic. This use of 'word' can also be found in Psalm 147:15,18,19, where God's word is also the law revealed to Israel.

Secondly, in the prophets, the word of God not only conveys truths and predicts the future; it also moulds history. When spoken by a prophet, the word of God enacts judgements (Is 9:7ff), gives new life (Ezek 37), creates a new and effective covenant (Jer 31:31ff). The whole body of revealed law (spoken by God through Moses) is the voice of God, accessible 'in your mouth and in your heart for you to put into practice' by dialogue with God (Deut 30:11-14).

At the incarnation, this Logos of God became 'flesh' – utterly human, frail and mortal, as Jesus the Christ, the only Son of God. Thus Jesus is both the creative love of God and also the perfect, fully human response to it. He reveals God, makes God accessible as never before, offers us the fullest possible relationship and dialogue with God, and restores the harmony between God and his universe.

That harmony rests on the pre-existent harmony between the Father, the Son (the Word) and the Holy Spirit. It is illuminating to start from John's report of the final words of Jesus on the cross, 'It is fulfilled' (Jn 19:30), which is 'tetelestai' in the Greek, from the word which means that something has reached its perfection or purpose. If we then ask when 'it' started, our thoughts get pushed back to where John starts his Gospel: 'In the beginning was the Word: the Word was with God and the Word was God.' In everything that Jesus does and says between that beginning and that end he shows that nothing whatever can move him away from his commitment to the Father, not even rejection, degradation and death. The crucifixion is the final proof of that; but everything which has preceded that final moment of his earthly life also shows the same dedication, the same spirit of sacrifice.

The heavenly harmony of God has been made flesh in Jesus the Christ, and he has shown that nothing can break that harmony. He has brought God's pattern of wholeness into the creation again as God had originally intended. But 'the Word made flesh' is far more than the restoration of an original harmony long since broken by mankind's bid for independence; Jesus the Word comes as the climax of history, not the beginning of it. He is the final stage of the universe, where God always intended that it should finish. And he is also the beginning of a new creation which began with

Jesus' cry 'It is fulfilled' at the moment of death and the empty tomb of his resurrection.

As we have seen, John's Gospel is written to a different plan from the other three and in a quite different style. John provides his key to Jesus in the opening chapter, where he announces that Jesus is the Word of God made flesh, the divine agent of cosmic creation who already existed when the universe was made. But that opening passage also links Jesus with judgement, for 'his own people' refused to accept him, but those who did accept him become children of God (Jn 1:1-13). Jesus as the final judge of the world is a recurrent theme in John's Gospel, which reaches its climax with the events of the final week and the crucifixion and resurrection.

These events themselves are the judgement. At the beginning of that week when Jesus committed himself to all that was going to happen during it, John reports that Jesus said, 'Now is the judgement of this world, now shall the ruler of this world be cast out; and I, when I am lifted up, will draw all men to myself' (Jn 12:31f). Here again the crowds listening to Jesus were in no doubt about his meaning, for they immediately began to ask him what kind of Messiah would let himself be crucified and die. Jesus answered them not with an explanation but with a warning of judgement. Their future depended, he said, on how they received him, and they had very little time left: 'Walk while you have the light, lest the darkness overtake you... While you have the light, believe in the light, that you may become sons of light' (Jn 12:35f).

The journeys of Jesus and the Holy Spirit

In Luke's two volumes, the Gospel and the Acts of the Apostles, the action is developed in terms of journeys and the work of the Holy Spirit. 'Journey' itself is a strong biblical image for the development of God's plan of salvation towards its triumphant fulfilment. The definitive origins of this concept lie in the Hebrews' exodus journey from slavery in Egypt through the Red Sea to Mount Sinai and the covenant, then through the wilderness to the promised land 'flowing in milk and honey'. In that escape and journey, God showed his power to rescue his people and defeat all their enemies.

The exodus also provided the Hebrews with evidence that God had sent his Spirit to work amongst them, the same Spirit which had hovered over the face of the primeval chaos when God created the universe itself (Gen 1:2). It was by God's Spirit that Moses, the priests and the elders of the people were able to lead them and reveal God's will to them during the long years of the exodus journey.

God's outpouring of his Spirit is an equally strong element in the prophetic descriptions of the cataclysmic events of the 'last days' when God will come in judgement:

> 'I will pour out my spirit on all flesh;
> your sons and your daughters shall prophesy;
> your old men shall dream dreams,
> and your young men shall see visions.
> Even upon the menservants and the maidservants
> in those days I will pour out my spirit.
> And I will give portents in the heavens
>   and on the earth,
> blood and fire and columns of smoke.
> The sun shall be turned to darkness,
> and the moon to blood,
> before the great and terrible day of the Lord comes'
>   (Joel 2:28-31).

The journeys in Luke's Gospel weave together Jerusalem, Nazareth and Bethlehem; then they follow the events in Jesus' public ministry from his first actions 'with the power of the Spirit in him' in Galilee, through to the climax in Jerusalem; and then they trace the spread of Christianity in the Gentile world until it has reached Rome, the new centre of the civilised world. These journeys represent the dynamic of God's power, the irresistible work of the Holy Spirit, as

God establishes his rule over the world through his Son. But they also indicate that the events involving Jesus and his followers are the start of the final stage of all God's plans for his creation.

The journey sequence begins with Mary, pregnant with Jesus by the Holy Spirit, travelling from Nazareth to Judah, the traditional Jewish heart-land, to visit her cousin Elizabeth, pregnant with the child who will become John the Baptist, herald of Jesus the 'Christ' or Messiah. In the next journey, Mary and Joseph travel from Nazareth to Bethlehem, just south of Jerusalem, which was King David's birthplace and the ancestral centre of the tribe of Judah, and Jesus was born while they were there.

From Bethlehem, the journey continues to the Temple in Jerusalem, so that Joseph and Mary may offer the minor sacrifice prescribed by the Jewish ritual law after childbirth. There, at the most sacred place on earth for Jews, Simeon proclaims Jesus as the Saviour of both Gentiles and Jews, in words familiar to Jews from the prophet Isaiah. The narrative returns the family to the obscurity of Nazareth, to end a journey in which Luke had drawn together all the main features of Jewish hopes, even the extension of the ancient covenant to include all peoples.

The next journey occurs when Jesus reached the age of twelve and goes with his family to Jerusalem for the feast of Passover and Unleavened Bread. Luke makes the main point about this journey through his first recorded words of Jesus: 'Did you not know that I must be in my Father's house?' (Lk 2:49).

The next, and final description of a journey in Luke's Gospel begins at 9:51, after the baptism, temptations and Galilean ministry of Jesus, and occupies nearly ten chapters.

Luke provides the essential clue to this journey's significance at the beginning of it: '...as the time drew near for him to be taken up, he resolutely turned his face towards Jerusalem.' In that phrase the crucifixion, resurrection and ascension are combined into one event, and everything which happens during the journey is a comment about it. So what appear to be comparatively mundane incidents take on a new significance.

This final journey is packed with descriptions of encounters, teaching, parables and miracles. And all of it is commentary on the kind of life which Christians should follow as a consequence of the death, resurrection and ascension of their Lord, Jesus the Christ. They are now living in the new Messianic Age which Jesus has inaugurated, filled with the Spirit he has poured out on them, and they will be judged by the standards of this new life of the Spirit, not the old life from which they have been saved.

When Luke's references to the Holy Spirit are examined, the most important are seen to be the three occasions when he describes Jesus receiving the Holy Spirit: first to effect his conception (Lk 1:35); then at his baptism, when his public ministry began (Lk 3:22); and finally at his exaltation as Lord of the universe, at his resurrection and ascension (Acts 2:33). Each of these marks the start of a new phase in Jesus' fulfilment of the divine plan.

Other references to the Holy Spirit show a wide range of effects arising from the Spirit's involvement in events, amongst the people of the Old Testament as well as in the work of Jesus and the people associated with him. Most important of these is the general description of the results of receiving the Spirit, quoted by Jesus from Isaiah 61 in the synagogue at Nazareth: good news given to the afflicted, liberty to captives, sight to the blind, freedom to the oppressed and the proclamation of the arrival of God's promised golden age.

John the Baptist is filled with the Spirit 'even from his mother's womb' so that he can fulfil his role as the new Elijah, the forerunner of the Messiah. The Spirit inspires Elizabeth to greet Mary as 'the mother of my Lord', and moves Zechariah to utter the *Benedictus* and Simeon the *Nunc Dimittis*. The Spirit fills Jesus with joy at the success of his disciples on their first mission.

The apostles are baptised with the Holy Spirit and empowered to be witnesses to Jesus 'to earth's remotest end', to be understood by people of many languages, and to speak boldly when they are brought before judges. These same gifts are extended to all believers, whatever their status: slaves, men and women, Gentiles, Cornelius and his household who receive 'the identical gifts he gave to us', and the believers in Ephesus. Jesus chooses the apostles 'through the Holy Spirit'; Paul's blindness is removed by the Spirit after his conversion. The Spirit asks for Barnabas and Saul (Paul) to be set apart for their mission, and makes overseers of local Churches. It is the Spirit, in association with the apostles, who decides that Gentile converts do not need to keep the Mosaic Law, binding on all Jews.

The Spirit leads Jesus into the desert for the temptations, and transports Philip to Ashdod from the Gaza road. During the second mission Paul and Timothy are prevented by the Spirit from taking the route they had planned, and the Spirit leads Paul captive to Jerusalem at the end of his third mission.

People are taught what to say. The Spirit inspires 'the disciples at Tyre' to tell Paul not to go on to Jerusalem, and inspires the prophet Agabus to tell Paul that he will be bound as a prisoner. The Spirit prompts what Stephen should say to his accusers, directs Peter's attention to the messengers from Cornelius and tells him to go with them. Visions and dreams are received, as promised by the prophet Joel; the Spirit rocks a house as people pray.

To sum up, Luke made it clear that by pouring the Spirit on his followers at Pentecost, Jesus associates them with his exaltation and with his messianic rule of the universe. Moreover, all believers similarly share in the new powers through baptism, and in the new responsibilities given to the apostles. Looking back, as he wrote the Acts of the Apostles some fifty years after the crucifixion, Luke attributed the whole growth of the Church to the outpouring of the Holy Spirit by the risen and ascended Jesus. The crucifixion, resurrection and ascension of Jesus had been the climax of world history, and the start of the new Messianic Age in which Luke and his readers believed they were already living.

The infancy stories

Only Matthew and Luke give the story of the birth and infancy of Jesus, the Christmas story, but although their accounts of the early years of Jesus only occupy two chapters of each of these Gospels they are rich in the symbolism associated by Jews and the first Christians with the final Messianic Age.

Both Matthew and Luke list the ancestors of Jesus (Mt 1:1-17; Lk 3:23-38), but with different emphases and with variations in the names of the actual ancestors they list. Matthew emphasises Abraham, to whom the first Hebrew covenant was given by God, David, the first successful Hebrew king and the main model for the Messiah, and the end of the great exile of the Hebrews in Babylonia when the Temple was rebuilt in Jerusalem. The list is arranged in equal numerical sections to indicate God's single, developing plan of salvation, which comes to its climax with Jesus.

Luke places his list of Jesus' ancestors at the beginning of Jesus' public ministry and starts the list at an earlier point than Matthew's, with Adam himself. For Luke, Jesus is the new Adam, the new beginning of a new creation and the Saviour of the whole world. There is a similarity here with the surprising ending of the Book of Revelation, where God creates a new universe.

The theme of Messianic kingship emerges again in its full form in the infancy stories with Bethlehem, which was the birthplace of King David. The symbolism is stated most clearly and dramatically in the message of the angel Gabriel to Mary about the conception of Jesus:

'He will be great, and will be called the Son of the
  Most High;
and the Lord God will give to him the throne of
  his father David,
and he will reign over the house of Jacob for ever;
and of his kingdom there will be no end' (Lk 1:32f).

All the responsibilities and achievements of King David are turned into signs pointing to Jesus as the final agent and consummation God's plan of salvation: he delivers God's people from their enemies; his reign is eternal; he brings in a new covenant; he is guardian of God's peace which nothing can threaten.

John the Baptist, the cousin of Jesus whose conception and birth runs parallel to that of Jesus himself, is destined to go before Jesus 'in the spirit and power of Elijah' (Lk 1:17). The allusion here is to a prophecy by Malachi that the prophet Elijah would return as the herald of the Messiah immediately before the Day of Judgement: 'Behold, I will send you Elijah the prophet before the great and terrible day of the Lord comes' (Mal 4:5).

Another rich collection of Messianic prophecies is brought into the scene when Matthew quotes the 'Emmanuel' passage from Isaiah: 'Behold, a virgin shall conceive and bear a son, and his name shall be called Emmanuel' (Is 7:14). The Hebrew word 'Emmanuel' means 'God is with us', which seems obvious enough if Jesus is indeed Son of God; but in Isaiah this prophecy leads straight into great Messianic passages about divine judgement and punishment for God's enemies, and of salvation and glory in a new creation for all who remain faithful to him. These also apply to Jesus, the newly born 'Emmanuel'.

The parables

The four Gospels are statements about the absolute power of God, embodied in Jesus Christ to make salvation available to a human race made helpless by its own sin. But running all through the Gospels is a complementary theme: the need for faithful cooperation with God. Salvation requires free and loving response to God's freely offered love.

This is one of the strongest themes in the teaching given by Jesus, particularly when he used parables. Indeed, the very method of teaching by parables requires the cooperation of the listener, because the listeners have to draw their own conclusions from the parables. These conclusions challenge the listeners' existing beliefs, and make them think again. Eventually, Jesus wants them to accept his view of what is the true reality about God and the way that God's plans for his creation are developing.

All this can be seen by looking at some of the parables and the conclusions Jesus expected his listeners to draw from them. Matthew's Gospel contains many parables whose explicit subject is 'the kingdom of God', the Messianic society which Jesus has come to found; these are indicated in the list below with a (K). This does not imply that the other parables do not apply to the Messianic kingdom; all the teaching of Jesus, and all his actions relate to the Messianic kingdom of the final times, for he is the Messianic king.

Mt 5:14	The candle and the bushel
Mt 7:24	The houses built on rock and sand
Mt 9:16	The new patch on an old garment
Mt 9:17	The new wine in old wineskins
Mt 13:3	The sower
Mt 13:24	The weeds in the wheat (K)
Mt 13:31	The mustard seed (K)
Mt 13:33	The leaven and the lump (K)
Mt 13:44	The treasure hidden in a field (K)
Mt 13:45	The pearl of great price (K)
Mt 13:47	The dragnet (K)
Mt 18:12	The lost sheep
Mt 18:23	The unmerciful servant (K)
Mt 20:1	The labourers in the vineyard (K)
Mt 21:28	The two sons (K)
Mt 22:2	The marriage feast (K)
Mt 25:1	The ten virgins (K)
Mt 25:14	The talents (K)

The parables teach that the kingdom comes in an unexpected way and an unexpected form: it is like a large tree which grows from insignificant beginnings (the mustard seed) and at an unexpected time (the ten virgins with lamps). It contains unexpected people, at least for the time being, and it must be left to God to judge who should be allowed to belong to it (the weeds in the wheat; the dragnet). God's invitation to belong and his reward for those who respond may well offend the world's ideas about the way people should be rewarded for their services (the labourers in the vineyard).

God expects the members of his kingdom to risk everything that they value in order to gain entry to it (the treasure hidden in a field; the pearl of great price). Members must live by God's values, and treat others with the same generosity and forgiveness they themselves have received from God (the unmerciful servant).

Membership cannot be earned, it is by God's invitation and is only available to those who respond to the invitation (the marriage feast). Those who only appear to respond to God's call will be repudiated by God, but the invitation remains open to those who at first seem to reject God's call and only respond to it later (the two sons). Even if the Messianic kingdom is unrecognised, its presence can still permeate the whole of society and affect it (the leaven and the lump).

Jesus himself is the Son of God and Messianic king of God's kingdom, yet he is rejected by the religious leaders and teachers, the very people God has appointed to guard his revelations and to welcome the Messiah when he comes. They will even kill him in order to protect their power and privileges, but God will certainly overthrow them and give their honours to others in his kingdom (the wicked husbandmen).

Although the other parables do not explicitly mention the kingdom, as already noted, they reinforce and expand the message of the parables which do. The members of the kingdom must make it known to all the world (the candle); nothing will endure unless it is based on the teachings of Jesus (the houses built on rock and sand); the kingdom will be something quite new, rather than a continuation of past institutions (the new patch; the new wine); it will only expand and be effective where God finds the right conditions for it and the right response (the sower); God will spare no effort to reach those who seem lost to him (the lost sheep).

Such parables can be interpreted in three ways, and all three ways are viable when it comes to deciding whether or not the Messianic kingdom is here already. They can be read to mean that the kingdom has already come with the birth of Jesus Christ, the Messianic king, for the kingdom is where the king is. They can also mean that the kingdom is the Church, which came into existence after Jesus the Christ had entered into his glory and sent the Holy Spirit on his disciples at Pentecost. They can even mean that the kingdom will not come until the events of the last days occur: the final destruction of all powers opposed to God, the last judgement, the end of the world and the new creation.

This is the time to remind ourselves that God's revelation is a mystery beyond human understanding and certainly beyond human language. Whether the Messianic age has already come or still lies in the future, Jesus is the way to it, the truth of it and the new life available in it, and he is utterly accessible to all.

3

The climax of the Gospels

To the uninformed observer, the events of the final week of Jesus' life merely mark the tragic failure of a charismatic religious leader who had become too popular. Such an observer would decide that Jesus had overreached himself and that the consequences were inevitable: the nation's religious leaders concluded that his claims were blasphemous and that the crowds who flocked to him were a potential threat to law and order. Admittedly, the country was under the control of a foreign power, but the nation's rulers – religious and secular – were experienced politicians who could secure the execution of Jesus if they thought it was in the national interest for him to be destroyed. They did so, and subsequently dismissed the stories of his resurrection as groundless rumour spread by Jesus' disciples.

For those who believe that Jesus was – and is – the Messianic Son of God, the death and resurrection are evidence of something dramatically different from anything else that has ever happened. To Christians, the death and subsequent glorification of Jesus was the victory over evil which marked the beginning of the new and final era of God's rule. All the information in the gospels has been selected and arranged to support and explain these beliefs.

This function of the material in the earlier part of the gospels can be seen most clearly in the accounts of the miracles. As John explicitly states in his gospel, they are signs pointing towards the decisive events of the last week of Jesus' life. (The miracles are examined more thoroughly in my *The Miracles of Jesus*, a companion book to this one, so the subject will only be summarised here.)

The four gospels report that Jesus performed various kinds of miracles in the course of his public ministry: miracles which showed that he possessed extraordinary powers over nature; miracles of healing, some of which were accompanied by exorcism; miracles in which people were raised from death. All of them point forward to the crucifixion and resurrection, and all of them tell us something about the character of Jesus. Four main kinds of miracles are reported in the gospels:

	Matthew	*Mark*	*Luke*	*John*
1. Nature Miracles				
The Great Catch of Fish		5:4-10		
Another Catch of Fish				21:6-11
The Coin in a Fish's Mouth	17:24-27			
Feeding the 5000	14:13-21	6:30-44	9:10-17	6:1-14
Feeding the 4000	15:32-39	8:1-10		
A Fig Tree Cursed	21:18-22	11:12-14, 20-24		
The Storm Stilled	8:23-27	4:35-41	8:22-25	
Walking on Water	14:22-33	6:45-52	6:16-21	
Water Changed to Wine				2:1-11

2. Healings accompanied by the exorcism of demons

A Blind & Dumb Man	12:22			
The Canaanite Woman's Daughter	15:21-28	7:24-30		
A Dumb Man	9:32-33		11:14	
The Epileptic Boy	17:14-17	9:14-21	9:37-43	
The Man or Men of Gerasa (Gerasene Swine)	8:28-34	5:1-20	8:26-39	
The Man in a Synagogue in Capernaum		1:23-28	4:33-37	
(Mary Magdalene)		16:9	8:2	
The Woman Bent Double in a Synagogue			13:10-17	

3. Healings with no mention of exorcism of demons

Blind Bartimaeus	20:29-34	10:46-52	18:35-43	
A Blind Man at Bethsaida		8:22-26		
A Man Born Blind			9:1-7	
Two Blind Men	9:27-31			
The Centurion's Servant	8:5-13		7:1-10	
A Deaf-Mute		7:31-37		
A Dropsical Man			14:1-6	
A Leper	8:1-4	1:40-45	5:12-16	
Ten Lepers			17:11-19	
Peter's Mother-in-Law	8:14-15	1:29-31	4:38-39	
A Paralysed Man in Capernaum	9:1-8	2:1-12	5:17-26	
A Paralysed Man at Pool of Bethzatha				5:1-9
The Slave of the High Priest			22:50-51	
The Son of an Official at Capernaum				4:46-54
A Man with a Withered Hand	12:9-14	3:1-6	6:6-11	
A Woman with an Issue of Blood	9:20-22	5:23-34	8:43-48	

4. Raising the Dead

Jairus' Daughter	9:18-26	5:21-43	8:40-56	
Lazarus				11:1-44
The Son of a Widow at Nain			7:11-17	

The nature miracles indicate that Jesus was the divine agent of creation. As John makes clear at the beginning of his gospel, the universe had been made through Jesus; it was still being sustained through him, and Jesus would be the divine agent of God for bringing the whole creation to its ultimate end. He calmed the storm and walked on the waters, just as the first account of creation in Genesis depicted God imposing order on the waters of the chaos, and described the power of God hovering over the face of the waters.

This power was demonstrated in the crucifixion and resurrection when Jesus overcame death and rose to a new life and a new creation. This new life of union with God in the new creation is shared by Christians in the Eucharist, the 'Lord's Supper' instituted by Jesus on the night before the crucifixion. When the gospel writers recorded the miracles in which Jesus fed the hungry crowds, they carefully described how Jesus took bread, blessed God over it, broke it, and gave it to the disciples to distribute to the people. This pattern, repeated in the Eucharist, emphasised what the Eucharist really is: no less than the Messianic banquet of the new creation.

The miracles of exorcism show Jesus defeating evil of every kind, whether it appeared in solitary or multiple form, whether in Jesus' presence or at a distance, whether in Jewish or Gentile territory. The apostles and first Christians believed that Jesus finally subjected himself to the full force of evil by allowing himself to be crucified, and that his resurrection demonstrated that God's power was superior to anything that evil could do. The powers of evil had made their final, supreme effort to win the decisive victory in their war against God, and they had been defeated.

There were many miracles where Jesus brought people back to life again, or restored their bodies and minds to full health. When Jesus submitted to death by crucifixion he accepted a form of execution which was deliberately designed to destroy the body's faculties slowly and systematically. The gospels emphasise that the body of the risen Jesus was the same body that was executed, bearing the wounds of crucifixion and the final thrust of the soldier's spear. Jesus demonstrated in his own body that his risen life was a healing of the whole person and the full range of human faculties.

The prophets had taught that when the final 'Day of the Lord' came, the Messiah would not only defeat and punish his people's enemies, he would also restore the injured bodies of the sick and diseased:

'For behold the day comes, burning like an oven, when all the arrogant and all evildoers will be stubble; the day that comes shall burn them up, says the Lord of hosts, so that it will leave them neither root nor branch. But for you who fear my name the sun of righteousness shall rise, with healing in its wings. You shall go forth leaping like calves from the stall... on the day when I act, says the Lord of hosts' (Mal 4:1-3).

Jesus first demonstrated the fulfilment of this Messianic promise in his own risen body. 'This is the day which the Lord has made' is the great cry of rejoicing in the Easter liturgy. It celebrates the resurrection of Christ as the start of the new creation where all humanity can be healed and made whole, body and soul.

The hour of Jesus

Literally speaking, 'hour' is just a conveniently small unit of time, a subdivision of a day which now has a standard, defined length of 60 minutes and 3,600 seconds, which we all accept without thinking. But the word is also used as an idiom we all understand, meaning the culmination or climax of a development, the moment it has all been leading to when we shall know success or disappointment: 'the hour has come'.

In his carefully structured Gospel, John reports that Jesus used the word 'hour' in this latter sense on a number of occasions. The first time was right at the beginning of his ministry when he used the word to refer cryptically to his death and resurrection; the last occasion was in his final prayer in the Upper Room just before leaving for the Garden of Gethsemane and his arrest.

That first occasion occurred during the wedding at Cana of Galilee when Mary, the mother of Jesus, told him during the festivities that there was no more wine left. Clearly, she expected him to do something about it. Jesus replied to her ambiguously, but implied that whatever surprising powers he now revealed in order to save the situation, it did not mean that this was the moment of Messianic rule: 'My hour has not yet come,' he said (Jn 2:4), but he immediately told the servants to fill the great water jars and he then quietly turned the water into wine. Jesus certainly exercised his Messianic powers, but this particular event was only the first 'sign', says John, pointing to who Jesus really was. It was not yet the 'hour' of decisive, final action when God would reveal Jesus in his full power.

The second occasion when Jesus referred to the coming 'hour' was during his conversation with the Samaritan woman at the well at Sychar. She told him that Samaritans saw no need to go to the Temple in Jerusalem to worship because they had their own holy mountain, and Jesus replied that 'the hour is coming when neither on this mountain nor in Jerusalem will you worship the Father'; he added that 'the hour is coming, and now is' when the Father could be worshipped in spirit and truth (Jn 4:21,23). The woman knew that such an hour depended on the arrival of the Messiah, and Jesus revealed to her that he indeed was the Messiah. But this was not yet the final and definitive revelation of Jesus; that was yet to come in Jerusalem and in a way none of his followers expected.

Jesus returned to his home in Galilee, and then went alone to Jerusalem for one of the festivals. There he healed a paralytic at the pool of Bethzatha near the Temple. It was a Sabbath day, and during the subsequent confrontation with rigidly orthodox Jews Jesus told them that he was the Son of God who had been given power by the Father not only to heal but to give life to the dead: 'The hour is coming, and now is, when the dead will hear the voice of the son of God, and those who hear will live...' (Jn 5:25). In the course of a long statement, Jesus went on to say that he was also the judgement of all those listening to him, because they were refusing to come to him for life.

The Messianic claims Jesus was now making were becoming more and more explicit, and he was also emphasising that the final Messianic judgement of the world was at hand. The next time Jesus went to Jerusalem for a festival, again without his disciples, he made his Messianic claims openly in the Temple courts and the authorities made plans to arrest him. John explained, however, that 'no one laid hands on him, because his hour had not yet come' (Jn 7:30).

Even when Jesus repeated his claims shortly afterwards, in a confrontation with Pharisees who certainly recognised what he was claiming, 'no one arrested him, because his hour had not yet come' (Jn 8:20). Such restraint by the authorities may have seemed like prudence in the face of Jesus' public popularity, but to those who really understood it was because God knew that the time had not yet come for the final confrontation.

Eventually Jesus announced that the time had finally come. He had already displayed the traditional symbols of the Messiah during his formal entry into Jerusalem, and in making the announcement he linked this triumphal entry with his approaching death:

'The hour has come for the Son of man to be glorified. Truly, truly, I say to you, unless a grain of wheat falls into the earth and dies, it remains alone; but if it dies, it bears much fruit...

Now is my soul troubled. And what shall I say? Father save me from this hour? No, for this purpose I have come to this hour...' (Jn 12:23-27).

The climax of Jesus' use of 'hour' is reached in the Upper Room discourses, Jesus' final words of freedom at the Last Supper, immediately before he left for the Garden of Gethsemane and his arrest. In his introduction to these discourses John says that 'when Jesus knew that his hour had come to depart out of this world to the Father, having loved his own who were in the world, he loved them to the end' (Jn 13:1). Jesus was about to give Judas the instructions which gave him the opportunity to tell the authorities where they could safely arrest Jesus.

Jesus used the remaining time to prepare his disciples for what was about to happen, telling them that there would be great pain, like a woman in childbirth who 'has sorrow, because her hour has come' (Jn 16:21); but once the child is born, he said, she forgets the sorrow because of her joy. The Messianic triumph of Jesus would only come after he had demonstrated to the world his unbreakable resolve and his devotion to his role in the horrors and degradation of a crucifixion.

After that, it could be made clear to all who would listen that the events of the final times would be based on God's ideals of limitless love, not on mere human standards of justice and revenge. Meanwhile, however, Jesus warned his disciples that 'the hour is coming, indeed, it has come, when you will be scattered, every man to his home,' and Jesus would be left alone to his fate; the final victory would be won by Jesus alone without the help of his disciples (Jn 16:32).

Jesus himself then turned to the Father in prayer, which were to be his final words in the Upper Room, and those who overheard him were left in no doubt that the approaching sufferings would be part of the expression of Messianic glory:

> 'Father, the hour has come; glorify thy Son that the Son may glorify thee...
>
> I glorified thee on earth, having accomplished the work which thou gavest me to do; and now Father, glorify thou me in thy own presence with the glory which I had with thee before the world was made...' (Jn 17:1-5).

John reports that as the climax approached, Jesus' thoughts turned to the divine status he had laid aside at his conception and birth. This is how John's Gospel had started, that Jesus was the Word of God, the pattern and power revealed in the creation of the universe. And this was now the climax of God's intentions for the creation; its ultimate outcome was not to be the endless chaos of human sin, but the saving power of God's love incarnate in the crucified and glorified Jesus.

The final week and the eschatological discourses

The triumphal entry of Jesus into Jerusalem for the last time is one of the most familiar of all the scenes from the gospels, and each gospel in its own way leads carefully into it. Matthew's structure leads up to it with a series of sermons and discourses by Jesus; for Mark this event breaks the careful public silence Jesus has tried to maintain about being Messiah; Luke gives more than eleven chapters of material explicitly leading up to it; and John prepares for it with his careful selection of seven miracle-signs.

The occasion was carefully chosen by Jesus; it was four days before the greatest of the annual Jewish pilgrimage festivals when all Jews who could get there were required to gather in Jerusalem for the sacrifices at the Temple. This was the double feast of Passover and Unleavened Bread and Jerusalem would already be crowded. It commemorated God's act of redemption at the Hebrews' escape from Egypt (Ex 12-14), and all the other great festivals were linked to it.

Jesus not only chose the occasion, he also deliberately chose symbolic actions which every informed Jew would immediately recognise as Messianic. Hebrew tradition held that the Messianic battle at the end of history would take place on the Mount of Olives outside Jerusalem, and the victorious Messiah would enter Jerusalem in triumph, riding a donkey as a symbol that peace was now secure:

'Tell the daughter of Zion,
Behold, your king is coming to you,
humble, and mounted on an ass,
and on a colt, the foal of an ass' (Mt 21:5, quoting
    Zechariah 9:9).

Jesus duly entered Jerusalem from the Mount of Olives, riding on a donkey.

Led by Jesus' disciples, the crowds spread greenery from trees and garments to pave the way, and shouted Messianic titles and greetings to welcome Jesus: 'Hosanna to the Son of David!'; 'Blessed is he who comes in the name of the Lord!'; 'Hosanna in the highest' (Mt 21:9) and 'Blessed is the kingdom of our father David that is coming!' (Mk 11:10). These are quotations and echoes from the pilgrimage psalms (118:26) and from the popular Psalms of Solomon, which look forward to the final Messianic triumph. The Messiah would restore the Hebrew kingdom King David had founded a thousand years earlier, and would fulfil all its promises of lasting peace and glory. That was what the crowds now expected Jesus to do.

In Matthew's account, Jesus then went straight to the Temple, as was expected of the Messiah, and cleansed it of the extortionate trading and money-changing that went on in its courtyards. When challenged, Jesus replied with two familiar quotations from the prophets, one about the Temple becoming a centre where all nations would find God (Is 56:7), and the other a denunciation of religious leaders for their corruption (Jer 7:11): 'Is it not written, My house shall be called a house of prayer for all the nations? But you have made it a den of robbers!' (Mk 11:17). Jesus would have been arrested on the spot for those words, but he was surrounded by a sympathetic crowd.

During the next three days Jesus told three parables in the course of public argument, which emphasised his Messianic claims and his judgement of the nation's religious leaders. The parables were the Two Sons, the Wicked Tenants of the Vineyard, and the Marriage Feast (Mt 21:28-32, 33-46; 22:1-14; with parallels in Mk and Lk). His comments reached their climax in a long judgemental denunciation of the Scribes and Pharisees, and a lament over Jerusalem for the suffering it would experience because it was refusing to accept him (Mt 23:1-39 and parallels).

Jesus' Messianic claims and warnings during that final week come to a new climax with his great 'apocalyptic' discourse (Mt 24:3 – 24:3-51; Mk 13:3-37; Lk 21:7-36). It was stimulated by expressions of wonder from the disciples as they tried to get Jesus to go on a tour of the Temple with them. Jesus told them that its glories would soon be totally destroyed with not one stone left upon another. They all retreated to the Mount of Olives.

Gazing out over the splendours of the city, the disciples asked Jesus when his predictions would happen. His reply to them echoed the language of Jewish apocalyptic and anticipated the dire descriptions of the final book of the New Testament, the Book of Revelation.

First Jesus warned them that there would be false messiahs, international wars, earthquakes and other natural disasters. Those who remained loyal to Jesus as Messiah would be tried both by religious and by secular courts, betrayed by their closest relatives, tortured and executed. Nevertheless, the Messiah would eventually triumph, his message would be preached to the furthest ends of the earth and those who remained faithful would be saved.

Meanwhile, Judaea itself would experience desecration and destruction, said Jesus, which would be initiated by the sight of 'the desolating sacrilege spoken of by the prophet Daniel, standing in the holy place,' (Mt 24:15). This refers back to an incident in 167 BC during the Maccabean Wars of the Hebrews against the Greeks, when the Greeks had erected an altar to Zeus in the Hebrew Temple in Jerusalem and made it the official centre of worship (1 Macc 1:54; Dan 9:27). By the time of Jesus the incident had become a general term for any serious desecration.

When the final desecration happened, said Jesus, there would be no time to salvage any possessions; wherever they were and whatever they were doing, God's people should immediately flee to the hills and pray that the final disasters did not begin in winter or on a Sabbath, which would only increase their suffering. God would shorten this period of tribulation, said Jesus, or else no one could survive it. He again warned that there would be many claiming to be the Messiah, but they should all be ignored.

The real coming of the Messiah would be unmistakable, Jesus went on. He would be seen coming as the Son of Man on the clouds of heaven with power and great glory, heralded by angels who would gather God's faithful together from all over the earth (Mt 24:30f and parallels). 'The Son of Man' phrase alludes to a famous apocalyptic passage in Daniel (Dan 7 and 8), which describes a divine hero sent by God with an angelic army to defeat the powers of evil in a final battle and establish God's rule. Jesus would apply this passage to himself at his trial by the Hebrew supreme court, which promptly condemned him for blasphemy.

Jesus' discourse to his disciples on the Mount of Olives about the final times ends with a warning for them to keep careful watch and to be faithful in the duties God gave them. Then he reinforced his warning with three more parables: the Ten Virgins who had been hired to await the bridegroom with lamps, only five of whom had lamps still burning when he arrived; the Talents, with its condemnation of the servant who had not used his gifts profitably while his master was absent; and the judgement parable of the Sheep and the Goats with its familiar description of a shepherd sorting out his flock.

The final judgement would depend, said Jesus, on whether people had dealt with those in need as if they were Christ himself: 'Truly, I say to you, as you did it not to one of the least of these, you did it not to me. And they will go away into eternal punishment, but the righteous into eternal life' (Mt 25:45f). After his descriptions of national and international catastrophe, Jesus applied his warnings about the final times at a personal and individual level, and with the simplest reasons for God's final judgement. It will depend on the way people have responded to the needs of the deprived.

The last supper, the trials and crucifixion

The Jewish Passover meal was – and is still – a commemoration of the escape from Egypt and the covenant, the most decisive of all God's revelations of his saving power and of his sovereign choice of the Hebrews to be the centre of his rule on earth. Jesus transformed this meal into a new commemoration of his own death and resurrection as the new revelation of God's redemptive love.

One simple key to this, unfamiliar to us now, was the Jewish custom of starting the day at sunset. Consequently, the Last Supper, the arrest of Jesus, the trials and his death all take place within the same Jewish day, from sunset to the following sunset. In the course of this particular Passover meal with his disciples, Jesus used words which showed that he thought of it as the Messianic feast which celebrated the imminence of the kingdom of God: 'I have earnestly desired to eat this Passover with you before I suffer; for I tell you I shall never eat it again until it is fulfilled in the kingdom of God.' And giving them all wine, he said, 'I tell you that from now on I shall not drink of the fruit of the vine until the kingdom of God comes' (Lk 22:15-18; see also Mt 26:29).

Jesus also added to the traditional blessings at the beginning and end of the long meal in ways which gave it an entirely new significance related directly to his approaching death. At the initial blessing and distribution of bread, he added the words, 'This is my body which is given for you. Do this in remembrance of me;' and at the final blessing of wine after the meal, he added, 'This cup which is poured out for you is the new covenant in my blood' (Lk 22:19-20).

Both of these additions had sacrificial connotations in Hebrew worship, particularly when an animal was totally consumed by fire on the great altar before the Temple. The blood of the animal contained its life, the Hebrews thought, and it was sanctified by God so that it could purify anyone touched by it. Jesus turned this meal into a combination of the Passover meal and the Temple sacrifices, and related it so closely to his own death that those who shared in it were also sharing in his own sacrifice.

He told them, moreover, to go on doing it for his 'remembrance', and the powerful Hebrew word represented here means that a past event is 'recalled' so completely that later generations could share in it as effectively as those who were participants in the original event. The Messianic age had already begun with this meal; it initiated a new covenant ratified by sanctified blood (see Ex 24:3-8, for a similar rite ratifying the original covenant); and Jesus made it available as the way that all future generations of his followers could share in his sacrifice.

Next morning (but in the same Jewish day) at his trial before the Sanhedrin, the Hebrew high court, Jesus finally broke his silence when the High Priest asked him directly if he was the Messiah, 'the Christ, the Son of the Blessed.' 'I am,' said Jesus; 'and you will see the Son of Man seated at the right hand of Power, and coming with the clouds of heaven' (Mk 15:61f).

It was the strongest claim Jesus could have made within Jewish religious traditions, for it directed everyone present to the most powerful Messianic prophecies of the Old Testament in the Book of Daniel (Dan 7 and 8), and removed any ambiguity there might be about the title 'Son of Man'. The court immediately condemned him to death. The Jewish religious authorities had then to move the case into the local Roman court and even change the charge to get Jesus executed, but they had made the decision which set in motion the death of the Messiah.

As Jesus had already indicated, his death was the redemptive sacrifice which now replaced all other sacrifices, not the mere execution of an innocent religious teacher. Such thinking was foreign to Hebrew Messianic traditions, but the resurrection of Jesus would decisively change that for Christians. For them, the execution of the Messiah marked the start of the final times, the Messianic Age.

The resurrection and ascension

The gospels emphasise that the resurrection of Jesus was the moment when the Messianic community of the final times came into being, by the way they report the appearances of Jesus to his disciples after his resurrection and the instructions he gave to them. He convinced them that it really was the Jesus they had known and had seen die, but now he was transformed. When they returned to Galilee expecting to resume their old way of life, Jesus went to them and directed them towards their new responsibilities; he instructed them to spread the good news that the new age had arrived and to baptise all who accepted it; most importantly, he imparted the Holy Spirit to them, so central a feature of the Messianic expectations.

Then the risen Jesus left them in a manner which convinced them that he would no longer be appearing unexpectedly to them. His next appearance, they soon believed, would signify the end of the world and the final judgement, but that would be described in other New Testament documents.

4

The first Christians and their Letters

The Acts of the Apostles

The main thrust of the Acts of the Apostles has been examined in the section of the previous chapter headed 'The journeys of Jesus and the Holy Spirit'. Written by Luke, it carries on the story of the origins of Christianity where Luke's Gospel ends, at the ascension of Jesus. That is very significant, for the ascension is the outward sign indicating that Jesus had finished his work on earth and was taking up his role of Lord of the universe. Acts states clearly that the times between the ascension of Jesus and his second coming are only an interim period, to give the Church the opportunity of preaching the good news about Jesus throughout the world.

The apostles were still thinking in the limited political terms of Hebrew nationalism, and asked Jesus if he was about to restore 'the kingdom to Israel' (Acts 1:6). Characteristically, Jesus told them that such knowledge of times or seasons was not for them. They would soon receive power when the Holy Spirit came upon them, Jesus continued, and then they must get on with being his witnesses to the end of the earth. The Greek word here translated by 'end' is 'eschaton', which means the termination of the time left for earth's existence as well as its geographical limits.

Immediately after the ascension, Luke reports that two angels told the apostles that they should not be just standing there gazing up into heaven:

> 'While they were gazing into heaven as he went, behold, two men stood by them in white robes, and said, Men of Galilee, why do you stand looking into heaven? This Jesus, who was taken up from you into heaven, will come in the same way as you saw him go into heaven' (Acts 1:10f).

They received the Holy Spirit shortly afterwards, and the rest of Acts is the account of their work of witnessing to Jesus – not to 'the end of the earth' but at least as far as Rome. The message is clear: the rapid and continuing growth of the Church is the work of the Holy Spirit. Equally clearly, this is a sign that the final times have arrived, the beginnings of the Messianic Age. How these final times will end remains to be seen when Jesus comes again.

The first Christians' Letters and the Gospels

At this point it is important to remind ourselves that most of the Letters in the New Testament were written before any of the Gospels reached the developed form in which we now have them. The Letters are therefore our earliest source of information about the first Christians, their beliefs and their way of life.

To make full sense of this we need to remember how the New Testament first developed. The four Gospels as we now know them were not written until the second half of the first century. They are certainly the most important source of our information about Jesus, but they also reflect the experiences and beliefs of the first two or three generations of Christians. This can best be appreciated if we see the books of the New Testament along with the main events of their times (although there is wide agreement on the main outline of what follows, there is less agreement about some of the details):

AD 33	March: Crucifixion, resurrection and ascension of Jesus. May: Pentecost; the Holy Spirit comes to the apostles.
36	Martyrdom of Stephen; Conversion of Paul
45	Paul's first mission
48	Council of Jerusalem to decide if new Christians have to become Jews as well (Acts 15)
49-52	Paul's second mission *Letters: 1 & 2 Thessalonians*
53-58	Paul's third mission *Letters: Philippians; 1 Corinthians; Galatians; 2 Corinthians; Romans; Philemon*
58	Paul arrested in the Temple in Jerusalem
60-61	Paul goes to Rome for his legal appeal
61-63	Paul under guard in Rome *Letters: Colossians; Ephesians*
63-64	Paul freed; mission to Spain? *Letters: 1 Timothy; Titus; 1 Peter;* *Mark's Gospel*
64	Burning of Rome *Letter: 2 Peter*

	Peter martyred in Rome
66-70	Palestinian war between Rome and Jews *Letters: 2 Timothy; Hebrews*
	Paul rearrested and martyred
70	Destruction of Jerusalem by the Romans *Letter of James*
75	*Matthew's Gospel*
	Luke's Gospel and Acts
	Letter of Jude
90	*Letters: 1, 2 & 3 John*
	John's Gospel
95	Persecution under Emperor Domitian *Book of Revelation*
	End of the New Testament writings, because there is no longer anyone alive chosen by Jesus himself to bear witness to him.

Paul

By far the largest number of the Letters in the New Testament were written by Paul. Three main cultures of the first century AD Roman Empire meet in Paul, who was a Jew, a Greek and a Roman citizen. He used all these to interpret Christ to the members of the Churches he founded during his journeys through the areas of what is now Greece and Turkey.

As a Jew, Paul was a strict Pharisee trained in Jerusalem

as a rabbi-lawyer and was authorised by the Jewish supreme court to arrest Christians in Damascus for trial in Jerusalem. He was also Greek, born a citizen of Tarsus, a large, wealthy port and free city, and a famous centre of Greek scholarship. His sympathies towards the 'Greek' world of the ancient Middle East helped his missionary work. He inherited Roman 'citizenship' (hence his Roman name 'Paulus'), and was proud of it. The universal 'peace' and law within the Roman Empire certainly influenced the kind of language Paul used to teach about Jesus the Christ as Lord of the universe.

Above all for us, of course, Paul was a Christian. The descriptions of Paul's conversion on the road to Damascus (Acts 9:1-19; 22:6-16; 26:12-18) focus on Paul's conviction that he had experienced a vision in which the risen Jesus told him that his actions against the Damascus Christians amounted to persecution of Jesus himself, and called him to be an apostle.

This experience laid the foundation for the central points of Paul's subsequent preaching and teaching. Like any other convert, Paul received instruction in the teachings of Jesus by those who were already Christians, but he was also clear that the truth of this teaching came directly from Christ, and that all Christians are united with Christ himself. This union is the basis of the individual Christian's relationship to God, and also of all Christians' relationship with each other as a community (e.g. Rom 6:3-11; 12:4-10; 1 Cor 12:12-30).

In the course of his Letters to the Churches he founded or visited Paul draws on a number of analogies to indicate the nature of the Christian community. It is a plant sown by God and tended by the apostles; a temple of the Holy Spirit with Jesus as the foundation and the Christians as the stones; a body composed of many parts, all of them essential to its well-being. It is also a new Israel or holy nation; a bride whose husband is Christ. But whatever analogies Paul uses for the mystery of the Christian community, the risen and exalted Christ is central to all of them.

This belief in the existing community on earth of the exalted Christ is combined with the belief that this community has yet to attain to its complete and perfect form, which will only be reached in heaven after the second coming of Jesus:

> 'But our commonwealth is in heaven, and from it we await a saviour, the Lord Jesus Christ, who will change our lowly body to be like his glorious body, by the power which enables him even to subject all things to himself' (Phil 3:20f).

Paul was careful to make it clear that it is not possible to say exactly what the risen body will be like; it is enough to know that it will be appropriate to our risen state, spiritual, imperishable and glorious, like the risen body of Christ himself, and it is as certain as Christ's own resurrection (1 Cor 15:35-57).

Paul and the first Christians believed that they were living in the overlapping of the final stages of God's master plan for his creation, and Paul emphasises this in his Letters. They were already living after the events which inaugurated the new Messianic Age, Jesus Christ's death, resurrection and exaltation; and they were now waiting for the events which would complete the Messianic Age and bring the whole creation to perfection.

They had all been chosen by God before the world was even made, Paul wrote to the Christians of Ephesus, and destined by him to be his sons through the redemptive cleansing from sin that Jesus had achieved for them. They had received the Holy Spirit at their baptism as a guarantee of the inheritance God had in store for them when his plan for the universe reached its final fruition (Eph 1:3-14). It was a theme Paul expounded in many different ways throughout his Letters.

One consequence of this can be seen in Paul's teaching about the central act of Christian worship, variously called the 'Lord's Supper' or 'Breaking of Bread' in the New Testament, and subsequently called the Eucharist, or the Mass. Paul taught that in this act of worship Christians express their union with Jesus as his body, and share in his body and blood (1 Cor 10:16f), but he also relates it directly to the Second Coming of Jesus: 'For as often as you eat this bread and drink this cup, you proclaim the Lord's death until he comes' (1 Cor 11:26).

In a number of his Letters, whether they are early ones, such as the Letters to the Thessalonians, or later, such as Philippians, Paul refers explicitly to the Christian hope in the second coming of Jesus:

> 'The Lord himself will descend from heaven with a cry of command, with the archangel's call and with the sound of the trumpet of God.
>
> And the dead in Christ will rise first; then we who are alive, who are left, shall be caught up together with them in the clouds to meet the Lord in the air; and so we shall always be with the Lord' (1 Thess 4:16f).

Paul's description may be modelled on the state visit of an emperor to a provincial city, but it conveys convictions that were so clear to the first Christians that Paul had to warn them not to give up their jobs as they waited for Jesus to come.

One more point needs to be made about Paul's teaching and achievement, and that is his attitude towards the Hebrew law revealed in the Old Testament. Hope in the coming of the Messiah was central to the traditional Jewish teaching which Paul and the first Christians inherited from their Judaism, but the Old Testament linked these hopes to observance of the Mosaic Law. Paul taught firmly that no one can hope to achieve a right relationship with God by keeping laws – even laws revealed by God (like the Jewish law). 'Righteousness' and all that follows from it comes from sharing in Christ's righteousness as Son of God. Such a sharing is a free gift from God, through Christ and the Holy Spirit, and cannot be earned (Rom 3:21-26).

Paul's clear understanding of this became crucial as more and more non-Jews became Christians. At first such 'Gentile' converts were expected to accept all the obligations of the

Jewish law – in effect to become Jews, with Christianity as a form of Judaism. On this, Paul opposed Peter 'in public, because he was clearly wrong' (Gal 2:11-14), and the apostles eventually met and decided that gentile Christians were not obliged to keep the Jewish religious laws (Acts 15:1-34).

This decision marks the point when Christianity came into its own as a distinctive religious movement, and not a mere dissident sect of Judaism. It was made possible by Paul's clear understanding of the unique achievements of the crucified, risen and exalted Jesus. The Mosaic Law had served a vital purpose during humankind's spiritual infancy as a kind of tutor and guardian, Paul taught, but it was now superseded. In the Messianic Age there is no need for the limitations of Judaism or any other form of religious legalism and they must no longer be imposed.

Hebrews

Although very early on, important parts of the Church thought that the Letter to the Hebrews had been written by Paul, there were always doubts about this. Nowadays most accept that the differences in language and style make Pauline authorship very unlikely so that we cannot say with confidence who wrote it. This does not diminish its authority in any way and the Church accepted it as part of the scriptures before some of the other books of the New Testament.

More than any other book of the New Testament, except the Revelation to John, Hebrews emphasises the present glory and cosmic authority of Jesus 'in these last days':

> 'He reflects the glory of God and bears the very stamp of his nature, upholding the universe by his word of power. When he had made purification for sins, he sat down at the right hand of the Majesty on high, having become so much more superior to angels as the name he has obtained is more excellent than theirs' (Heb 1:3f).

And the author goes on to quote many Messianic passages from the Psalms to illustrate his meaning.

Hebrews gets its main insights into the Messianic age by comparing the risen and exalted Jesus with the high priests of the Hebrew religion. The main function of the Hebrew priesthood was to offer the animal sacrifices prescribed by the Mosaic Law, which is recorded in the books of the Old Testament from Exodus to Deuteronomy, and particularly in the twenty-seven chapters of Leviticus. The high priest presided over the whole priesthood, and he alone could enter the inner sanctuary, the 'holy of holies', where the Ark of the Covenant was housed. Long before the beginnings of Christianity the Hebrew religion had ruled that the sacrifices could only be offered in the Temple in Jerusalem, so all Hebrews had to go to the city to share in the round of sacrifices.

By his crucifixion, says the Letter to the Hebrews, Jesus had ended the need for the repeated animal sacrifices offered daily and on the great annual feasts. These were intended to purify the worshippers from any defilement which separated them from God, but Jesus had offered the supreme sacrifice of his own life once and for all. His blood shed on the cross now provided the ultimate cleansing from sin, and there was no need for any other sacrifice:

> 'It was fitting that we should have such a high priest (as Jesus), holy, blameless, unstained, separated from sinners, exalted above the heavens. He has no need, like those high priests, to offer sacrifices daily, first for his own sins and then for those of the people; he did this once and for all when he offered up himself' (Heb 7:26f).

This is the new covenant, says the author of Hebrews, which the prophets foretold for the final times when God would write his law on the hearts of his people so that they could respond spontaneously to his love; and Hebrews quotes the appropriate passage from Jeremiah (Jer 31:31-34).

At his resurrection and ascension, Jesus entered once and

for all into the ultimate holy place, heaven, taking with him his own blood to purify all who have need of redemption. So Jesus has already dealt with sin definitively, but he will appear a second time, says Hebrews, 'to save those who are eagerly waiting for him' (Heb 9:28).

Far from eliminating any need for the Last Judgement, this view of the achievement of Jesus intensifies it for Christians. In the early days of Christianity those who became Christians were adults who repented of their sins and were then baptised. They had accepted that Jesus was the Messianic Son of God who had given his life for them and purified them from their sins by his blood. If they then turned back to their old ways and sinned again they were consciously rejecting Christ's sacrifice and their only means of salvation:

> 'If we sin deliberately after receiving the knowledge of the truth, there no longer remains a sacrifice for sins, but a fearful prospect of judgement, and a fury of fire which will consume the adversaries... For we know him who said, Vengeance is mine, I will repay... It is a fearful thing to fall into the hands of the living God' (Heb 10:26-31).

There have been times in the Church's history when this passage has been applied not to God's Last Judgement, but has been interpreted as authority to condemn apostate Christians to a terrible death.

Hebrews ends with a description of the heavenly Jerusalem populated by angels, by those human beings who have already attained to heaven, by God the judge of all, and by Jesus (12:22-24). But this is no particular comfort, for this picture is presented as the hidden reality of Christianity; even though it is the place of the saving blood of Jesus, it is full of dangers for Christians who fail to acknowledge its presence properly: '...let us offer to God acceptable worship, with reverence and awe; for our God is a consuming fire' (Heb 12:28f).

The reason for these warnings probably lie in the terrible

reality of persecution in the very early years of Christianity, and the temptation to conform to the Roman empire's official cult of emperor-worship. Hebrews warns its readers that there is no permanent city for them here on earth; their security is only to be found in heaven, just as Jesus was crucified outside Jerusalem. Christians have to be ready to accept rejection and to find their salvation with Jesus in the heavenly reality outside the earthly city.

1 Peter

There is no doubting the reason for which the First Letter of Peter was written, for the author makes it quite explicit; they are enduring persecution. They can rejoice in the confidence that God's power is guarding them, even though,

> 'now for a little while you may have to suffer various trials, so that the genuineness of your faith, more precious than gold which though perishable is tested by fire, may redound to praise and glory and honour at the revelation of Jesus Christ' (1 Pet 1:6f).

They will inherit the grace, he says, for which the prophets searched. The image of being tested by fire like gold is taken from the techniques of the gold refiners, and the Gospels also use it about the temptations of Jesus Christ at the beginning of his public ministry. In the case of Jesus, the temptations demonstrated the strength of the power by which he was able to remain loyal to his mission; for Christians, persecution is an opportunity to experience and prove the power which can keep them loyal to Christ. Their scars become the hallmarks of their worth.

As in the Letters of Paul and the Letter to the Hebrews, the First Letter of Peter emphasises the relationships between baptism and the victory Jesus won over sin through his crucifixion and resurrection. Drawing on a well known Old Testament incident, but applying it imaginatively to the

Christian rite of initiation, the author points out that only very few believed in God at the time of the flood – Noah and his family – but they passed safely through the waters to salvation. So too with baptism,

> 'Baptism, which corresponds to this, now saves you, not as a removal of dirt from the body but as an appeal to God for a clear conscience, through the resurrection of Jesus Christ, who has gone into heaven and is at the right hand of God, with angels, authorities, and powers subject to him' (1 Pet 3:21f).

This is the key to the power available: that Jesus Christ is already reigning in supreme power with God, and that this power is now available through baptism.

Christians must live in the awareness that 'the end of all things is at hand', the letter continues (1 Pet 4:7). In this case the Greek word translated as 'end' is 'telos', which means the attainment of an ultimate objective, just as John used it in his Gospel to indicate the final word of Jesus on the cross just before he died. That was one objective Jesus reached, the victory on the cross over all that opposed his earthly mission; this is the complement of it, the extension by Jesus of that victory to all the universe and to all time.

Meanwhile, writes the author, Christians should be glad of the opportunity to share Christ's sufferings so that they can be equally glad when his final glory is revealed – provided only that they suffer innocently rather than because they are guilty of secular crimes. There speaks someone who is careful that Christians should not use their faith as a reason for lawlessness, a sensitive issue during the early days of Christianity within the Roman empire.

James

The Letter of James is different in tone to any of the other Letters of the New Testament, for it emphasises the importance of practical and apparently mundane social values for the Christian life, and relates these both to persecution and to the second coming of Jesus.

Where other books of the New Testament seem to lay their main emphasis on heroic virtues, James warns about keeping anger in check and the tongue under control. He emphasises that Christians should pay as much respect to the poor and unimportant as they do to the rich and well-dressed, and he does this at such length that such class consciousness must have been a conspicuous scandal when Christians met for worship. Paul delivers a similarly stern rebuke to the Christians of Corinth for the same fault when they meet for 'the Lord's Supper', and warns them that they will be eating to their own condemnation if they ignore what he says (1 Cor 11:17-34).

The reason for all this is clear, writes James, they are all awaiting the second coming of the Lord, like farmers waiting patiently for rain and the ripening of crops for harvest: 'establish your hearts, for the coming of the Lord is at hand' (Jas 5:8). It may seem mundane, but the coming of Jesus into this world, and what he achieved while he was in it, transformed mundane values into the courtesies of heaven. Whatever else they may do, the New Testament Letters demonstrate what a rich and varied range of concepts are contained within the teaching about the Last Days, the End times, the Messianic Age. But they do far more than that, for they tell us about the context of the faith and practice of the first generations of Christians, which forms the background for the four Gospels.

All the imagery and essential elements are there which eventually emerge in the detail of the Gospels: the fulfilment of the Old Testament's Messianic hopes; the new age brought in by the life, death, resurrection and ascension of Jesus; the significance of the Holy Spirit for the final times; the cosmic role of Jesus as Lord of the universe, the second coming of Jesus which heralds the final judgement and the new creation; the role of baptism as the entry into the new covenant and a share in the new life of the risen Christ.

Part 2:
THE BOOK OF REVELATION

5

Christ's judgement of the Churches
(Rev 1:1–3:22)

The prologue (1:1-3)

John's account of his visions starts with a declaration of their purpose. God sent them to him, says John, so that he could in his turn show God's servants what must soon take place. When John repeats this declaration near the end of his account, he adds an assertion that his words are true and can be trusted. John makes this assertion as an eye-witness of what he reports; they are visions, John emphasises, and he is reporting what he himself saw; an angel was sent to him, but the angel was only a messenger from God inviting John to receive the visions. Everything that John describes, he says, is on his own authority: 'I, John, am he who heard and saw these things' (Rev 22:8), and he also says that the angel reassured him that what he had seen and heard was true.

The point is important, for it has a direct bearing on how seriously these visions are to be taken. The answer for anyone who accepts the authority of the New Testament has to be, 'very seriously'. People plan their lives by what they hope – or fear – is going to happen, and John's visions open windows into what is really going on in the universe and what it is all leading up to. The language and imagery belong to John's own times and background, and a modern reader must translate it into language and imagery meaningful to our times and our background. But Christians are bound to believe that the truths that are being conveyed by this language and imagery are of the utmost practical importance for them.

It is hardly surprising, therefore, that John thinks that people who read these words and take them seriously are blessed, 'makarios' (1:3). This word is also used by Matthew to report the nine 'beatitudes' at the beginning of Jesus' Sermon on the Mount: 'Blessed are the poor in spirit...' (Mt 5:3-11). Later in his book, John repeats the blessings again and again with different reasons for them, very like Jesus had done: 'Blessed are the dead who die in the Lord..., is he who is awake..., are those who are invited to the marriage supper of the Lamb..., is he who shares in the first resurrection..., is he who keeps the words of the prophecy..., are those who wash their robes...' (16:15; 19:9; 20:6; 22:7,14). The number seven has a special significance for John, and there are seven of these beatitudes. Clearly, they all describe the people who take his message seriously and act on them.

The message and its source (1:4-8)

As we have seen, we may safely deduce that John was the chief pastor, 'archbishop' in our terms, of the Christian Churches in seven cities of what is now Asia Minor at a time of persecution. John's responsibilities towards his Christian flocks are never far from his mind throughout his visions, but they are right on the surface here at the beginning. The whole book is addressed especially to the seven Churches, and it comes to them with grace and peace from the divine source of the message, he 'who is and who was and who is to come' in conjunction with the Churches' seven guardian spirits and with Jesus.

Language like this expresses the realisation that God is beyond time. The language of time collapses. God 'is and was, and is to come'. St Augustine of Hippo put it another way when he said that we can only use the present tense to talk about God's eternal presence: 'God is not past as if he is not now, nor future as if he is not yet, for that which is eternal only ever is' (*Commentary on Psalm 2*). No matter what period of time we may be considering, past, present or future, God is present in it – and beyond all of them. That realisation should feed our prayers rather than confuse our thoughts; it should move us to adoration, the best way to begin prayer, rather than to speculation.

This realisation about God's eternity lay at the very heart of the Old Testament understanding of God. Old Testament writers identified it with the moment when Moses received his call from God, and this incident was probably running in John's mind as he began to write down his experiences. It is described in Exodus 3. The young Moses had fled from Egypt into the desert after killing an Egyptian who was beating a Hebrew slave. God spoke to Moses from a bush that was burning without damage, and told him to return to Egypt to rescue the Hebrews in God's name. When Moses asked God what his name was, he was told it was 'I am who I am... The Lord, the God of your fathers... This is my name for ever' (Ex 3:14-15). This word 'Lord' translates the Hebrew word 'Yahweh', which is derived from the continuous form of the verb 'to be' and was used by the Hebrews as the proper name of God. ('Jehovah' is another version.) God is unchanging and faithful for ever; that is all that Moses and his people need to know at present.

Jesus is coupled with this greeting as the faithful witness and first-born of the dead, who has freed us from our sins by his blood. In Hebrew worship the blood of a sacrificed animal was filled with God's life and power, so it could wash away the sins – at least the superficial ones – of anyone touched by it. As the supreme sacrifice, the blood of Jesus washes away all sin, writes John, and all who have been purified are made priests by Jesus to serve his God and Father. This promise lay at the heart of God's covenant to Moses and the newly liberated Hebrews immediately after their escape from Egypt: 'You shall be to me a kingdom of priests and a holy nation' (Ex 19:6). John is reminding his readers that this promise has been fulfilled in Jesus.

The seven spirits before God's throne are the guardian spirits of John's seven Churches. Later John saw them as seven torches burning before the throne of God (4:5). By bringing them into this opening greeting, John shows that God's message is a special one for each of the Churches, rather than something vague and general which can easily be ignored. Each spirit channels the vision to one local Church and applies it to that Church's particular situation and needs.

In these brief words John has laid the foundations for his book and he can now set out the purpose of it just as briefly. Jesus Christ 'is coming with the clouds, and every eye will see him' (1:7). His arrival will bring judgement on all who helped to kill him; for every tribe of people on earth will lament because of him. John does not say yet whether their weeping will be for what was done to Jesus, or for what is about to happen to them. All John's readers would know what he meant by Jesus 'coming with the clouds', for this image comes from a popular prophecy in the Book of Daniel about the 'son of man' coming on the clouds of heaven and being given eternal authority over all peoples (Dan 7:13-14). Jesus claimed this for himself at the decisive moment in his trial before the Jewish high court, and the claim led immediately to his condemnation for blasphemy (Mk 14:62).

John repeats his reminder of the eternal nature of God 'who is and who was and who is to come', coupled with another way of expressing it, 'I am the Alpha and the Omega' (1:8). These are the first and last letters of the Greek alphabet, and John was writing in Greek for his Greek-speaking readers. They would recognise it as a common metaphor for everything that exists, just as we might say 'A to Z'. And he adds another title for God, 'Pantocrator', which we translate as 'Almighty'. It comes originally from a word meaning 'strength', and then 'sovereignty', and it has the practical consequence that God is the actual ruler of the universe. All that follows in John's book will be a description of what that means in practice.

The opening vision (1:9-20)

John tells his flock that the visions started while he was on the Roman prison island of Patmos, which is in the Aegean Sea just off the coast of Asia Minor. John's seven Churches were nearby on the mainland. He was sent there, he says, 'on account of the word of God' (1:9), an allusion to his pastoral work, and he tells them that he is sharing their sufferings and their patience as well as their membership of God's kingdom.

John uses an intense word, 'synkoinonos', to link all this directly with Jesus. The word refers to people who all share something in common with each other, and in this case it is Jesus whom John and his people are sharing. They are sharing his sufferings, his endurance and his witness to God, and they are sharing in his kingdom. Paul also develops this theme powerfully near the beginning of his Second Letter to the Corinthians (2 Cor 1:3-7), and finds that sharing in the suffering of Christ gives access to the strength of Christ as well. Without that, endurance would be impossible. Christ himself demonstrated that no form of suffering could break his union with the Father. Like Paul, John is saying that the sufferings of Christ's followers is evidence – 'testimony' – that they are sharing in that union.

John says that he was praying in ecstasy one Sabbath when he heard a voice like a trumpet ordering him to record what he was about to see and send the book to his seven Churches. He turned and saw seven golden lampstands with 'a son of man' standing in their midst clothed in white and girded with gold. The figure held seven stars and had a sword pointing from his mouth; his face blazed like the sun at noon and his voice boomed like a great waterfall. John fell in fear at his feet.

The scene has echoes of a similar experience described in the Book of Daniel. There too the prophet had a vision of a white-clad figure girded with gold, and with the same blazing face and voice of power (Dan 10:5-19). As with Daniel, the figure told John not to fear, and he then identified himself as 'the first and the last and the living one' (1:17-18). John had just used this language of God, and the figure went on to indicate that he was the risen and glorified Christ: 'I died, and behold I am alive for evermore, and I have the keys of Death and Hades' (1:18).

Christ went on to explain that the seven lampstands were John's seven Churches, and the seven stars were their angels. Jesus had told his disciples that wherever two or three were gathered together in his name he would be present (Mt 18:20); John's vision of Christ standing in the midst of the seven Churches was a vivid confirmation of this promise.

Christ now ordered John to be his secretary, recording the messages Christ was sending to the seven Churches by their angels. Although each Church had its own special message from Christ, all the seven Churches were situated on the same major route and we can be sure that the whole of John's book of revelations would circulate among them.

The messages to the Churches (2:1-3:22)

The New Testament's Letters to the various Churches are outspoken when there are faults to be corrected. A modern reader of, say, Paul's First Letter to the Corinthians might well wonder how it was received by the Christians of Corinth when it was read out to them by their 'presbuteros', their minister or priest. The Letters to the seven Churches in the Book of Revelation are similarly outspoken; they give praise and encouragement where that is deserved or needed, but they also spell out the Churches' faults and warn them of the consequences.

John leaves no doubt about the authority behind the Letters, for it is Christ himself. Christ dictates the Letters to John. As he dictates Christ holds in his hand the seven stars which signify the angels of the seven Churches, and he walks among the seven golden lampstands which signify the Churches themselves. It is like the official visit of a supreme ruler inspecting cities under his rule and passing judgement on what he sees and hears. The first Church addressed is Ephesus, probably the largest of the seven as a city of a quarter of a million people and capital of the Roman province of Asia, where all seven towns were situated. The Letter congratulates the Christians of Ephesus for rejecting false teachers who claimed to be apostles.

According to Luke, author of the Acts of the Apostles, Paul had earlier warned the Ephesian Christians against 'fierce wolves' who would come among them, and divisive teachers from within their own Church (Acts 20:29-30). Now they were having to test such people against the Christian teaching they had received from John, while John himself was separated from them by his imprisonment. Moreover, their internal problems as a Church were connected in some way with the persecution they were experiencing.

They are also commended for rejecting 'the works of the Nicolaitans' (2:6). This may indicate what some of the false apostles were teaching: that it was permissible to eat food from the sacrifices in the various non-Christian temples which abounded in Greek cities, and to take part in the sexual acts which were a feature of the fertility religions (2:14-15).

Despite these words of approval by Christ, the Letter to Ephesus rebukes them for no longer loving Christ with the fervour they had first shown, and they are warned that their lampstand will be removed 'from its place' if they do not repent (2:5). Perhaps this means that they will lose their status as the chief Church of the province.

The letter ends with the assurance that anyone who conquers will eat from 'the tree of life, which is in the paradise of God' (2:7). This tree figures in the story of the Garden of Eden, together with the tree of the knowledge of good and evil (Gen 2:9), and eating from it conferred immortality. Adam and Eve were expelled from the Garden to deny them this opportunity (Gen 3:22-24). The tree of life appears again at the end of John's book, growing either side of the river of the water of life in the New Jerusalem (22:2).

Next comes the letter to the Christians of Smyrna from

Christ 'the first and the last, who died and came to life' (2:8). It contains no condemnations of them, only the reassurance that they need not fear what is about to happen to them. Some will be imprisoned and tested for ten days, says the letter, and some will die. The 'ten days' is an echo of the proof that Daniel gave, that he and his companions could survive on a restricted diet for ten days, and be fitter than those who had fed well. Applied to the Christians of Smyrna, it meant that those who suffered would be more fortunate than those who were spared.

One of the problems at Smyrna was slander by 'those who say they are Jews and are not, but are a synagogue of Satan' (1:9). Revelation is the only book in the Bible to contain this phrase, here and in the letter to Philadelphia (3:9), which became a favourite term of abuse among Christians at the Reformation. Here in Revelation it probably refers to Christians who claimed to be Jews so as to benefit from Jewish privileges within the Roman Empire. That raised great problems, particularly when they told fellow-Christians that they must keep the Jewish religious law. This controversy had been the first great internal crisis for the apostles, who had ruled firmly against the 'Judaisers' (Acts 15).

In this letter Christ tells the Christians of Smyrna that they are to be tested by the Devil, but if they are faithful it will secure them the crown of life; if they conquer they will not be hurt by 'the second death' (2:11). References to the second death occur later in Revelation, where it is a lake of fire into which a variety of sinners are thrown. It has no power over those who had remained faithful to Christ and refused to worship the beast (20:6; 21:8). The letter to Pergamum, which follows, identifies the author as Christ 'who has the sharp two-edged sword' (2:12), another feature of the majestic figure of Christ in the opening vision. The Christians of Pergamum were remaining loyal to Christ, even though their town was the throne of Satan. A faithful witness of Christ, Antipas, had been killed amongst them. The language used here suggests that Antipas had been executed by the Roman governor for being a Christian, and that Roman rule was Satanic. If this is the meaning, the language deliberately disguises it to avoid causing further trouble for the Christians.

Although they were remaining faithful under this threat, they were tolerating misleading teachers who followed the Nicolaitan beliefs, as in Ephesus. The letter uses Balaam, a Canaanite prophet, as a symbol of what is happening in their Church. As the Israelites approached the 'promised land' of Canaan after the exodus from Egypt, Balaam suggested that the Israelite threat could be neutralised by converting them to the Canaanite religion (Num 22-24). The Christians of Pergamum were like the Israelites, the letter implies, and they must resist or Christ would come amongst them with the sword of his mouth.

Those who conquer will receive the hidden manna and a new, secret name from Christ, the letter concludes. 'Manna' was the mysterious food by which God fed the Israelites during their journey across the desert after their escape from Egypt. The Exodus tradition says that God ordered a jar of the manna to be kept so that later generations of Israelites could see it (Ex 16:15-36). From this there arose a popular Jewish belief that the manna would be given again in the Messianic Age.

Closer to the hearts of the Christians of Pergamum would be the passage in John's Gospel where Christ said that he was the bread of life, the living bread which came down from heaven. The manna also came down from heaven, said Christ, but those who ate it still died; 'those who eat me will live because of me..., will live for ever' (Jn 6:49-58).

The Pergamum Christians would also receive a secret name, Christ promised, written on stone. In the Bible, a person's 'name' signifies his or her innermost personality, importance and authority; people are sometimes given new names when they are given radically new responsibilities by God. Here in this letter the secret new names represent the real character and destiny of those who are truly faithful. Only they themselves, and God, know who they are. There is an implicit warning here against judging other Christians, or of setting too much store by other Christian's judgements of oneself. The letter to Thyatira is introduced by more features drawn from the majesty of Christ revealed in the opening vision: 'The Son of God, who has eyes like a flame of fire, and whose feet are burnished bronze' (2:18). For the most part the message commends the members of this Church for their love, faithfulness, service and patience in the face of their sufferings. They are encouraged to hold firmly to what they have received, and to consolidate what they have achieved, until Christ comes.

These are the Church members 'who have not learned what some call the deep things of Satan' (2:24). But there are others among the Christians of Thyatira who had become involved with the Nicolaitan practices already condemned in sister Churches: taking part in pagan worship and the sexual rites of the fertility religions. The letter castigates their leader in terms of a notorious Old Testament character, Jezebel, whose name is still familiar nowadays as a term for a shameless woman and temptress. She was a Canaanite – the people of Palestine conquered by the Israelites – and wife of King Ahab of Israel during the turbulent years which followed the death of King Solomon. The Israelite histories depict her as a ruthless political figure who dominated her husband and led the Israelites astray with her native Canaanite religion, which featured human sacrifice and sacred prostitutes (1 Kings 18-21).

Only some of the members of the Thyatira Church had become followers of this teaching, but the letter accuses the rest of tolerating their leader. When Christ comes again it will be as judge. So far he has held his hand to give the 'Jezebel' of Thyatira time to repent but this opportunity has not been taken. If they do not repent now, says the letter, Christ will inflict terrible suffering on them, then kill them. Those who have remained faithful to Christ will share in Christ's own authority and help him to rule the nations, and Christ will give them 'the morning star'. This star is revealed as a symbol of Christ himself at the end of Revelation (22:16), so the gift shows how completely Christ the judge gives himself to those who are faithful to him. The Church in Sardis is told that its letter comes from 'him who has the seven spirits of God and the seven stars' (3:1), aspects once again of Christ in the opening vision of Revelation. Their message from Christ is a stern warning that he knows that they are dead even though they have a reputation for being alive. The Christians may have been too much influenced by the luxury and immorality for which their native city was notorious; if they do not repent and awake to their danger, says Christ, they will find his coming as unexpected as the visit of a thief in the night and as unwelcome.

Newly baptised Christians were given a white garment as they stepped out of the water after their immersion, and this custom provides the symbolism for the few Christians of Sardis who have remained faithful to what they received and heard. They have not soiled their garments, says their letter. They will walk with Christ in white and he will identify them by name to the Father in the presence of the heavenly court.

The symbols of Christ's authority for the Christians of Philadelphia do have an echo of the opening vision, but they are also a direct quotation from Isaiah. Christ is the one 'who has the key of David, who opens and no one shall shut, who shuts and no one opens' (3:7; Is 22:22). God's covenant with David made him and his descendants kings of Israel, administrators of God's law and the source of their people's security (2 Sam 7). This became the main model for the role and authority of the Messiah, and so – for Christians – of Jesus the Christ.

The Church in Philadelphia was also threatened by Christians who mixed their Christianity with pagan worship and the practices of the fertility religions, and who claimed the protection the Roman authorities allowed to Jews. The letter promises that Christ will make them prostrate to the faithful Christians and learn that it is they who are the ones whom Christ loves.

Because the true Christians have endured their sufferings faithfully they will be spared the sufferings that God is about to bring on the whole world, says Christ in his letter. Later in Revelation John describes his vision of the new Jerusalem descending from heaven (21:1–22:5); now the faithful of Philadelphia are promised that they will become pillars of God's temple and citizens bearing the name of the city of God and of Christ's new name. Here again, 'name' symbolises authority and status; this is a promise that ultimately the faithful will share Christ's own status in the new Jerusalem.

Laodicea, the final Church addressed, has become a byword for lack of enthusiasm as a result of their letter in Revelation, for Christ tells them that they are like lukewarm food and he will spit them out again. The titles for Christ at the beginning of this letter allude to the opening passage of John's Gospel, where Christ is the source of the new creation and the only perfect revelation of God.

The Laodicean Christians are secure and prosperous citizens whose Christianity contributes to their complacency. They have no sense of personal need, but in reality they are 'wretched, pitiable, poor, blind and naked' says Christ (3:18). They should look to Christ for refined gold and white garments, says their letter, and for eye ointment so that they may see properly.

The Laodicean Letter contains one of the most memorable, gentle and encouraging of all the images of Christ's love for his people: 'Behold I stand at the door and knock, if any one hears my voice and opens the door, I will come in to him and eat with him, and he with me' (3:20). Christ comes in judgement, but only those who finally reject every call of God's love will by condemned. This letter identifies these unfortunates as nominal Christians who feel secure and do not really acknowledge that they need Christ at all. They say, 'I am rich, I have prospered, and I need nothing' (1:17). They are terribly mistaken, as presumably they will discover when the persecutions sweeping the area catch up with them.

Those who conquer, this letter concludes, will sit enthroned with Christ, sharing the rewards of his own conquest. This promise echoes Paul's reassurance to the Christians of Rome, that they are heirs of God and fellow heirs with Christ, 'provided we suffer with him in order that we may also be glorified with him' (Rom 8:17). Despite their cryptic language, these letters to John's seven Churches have a startlingly modern ring. They depict Christians facing the moment of truth as they experience persecution, and their wide range of reactions to it. Some try to escape by claiming they are only a sect of Jews, entitled to the religious privileges accorded to Jews within the empire. For some, Christianity is just another ingredient in their religious stew, along with all the other religions of their region. Some have merely laid a shallow veneer of Christianity over their prosperous lives, perhaps as the current religious fashion amongst their set. And some are prepared to die rather than abandon or even compromise their faith in the crucified and risen Christ.

To all these Christ presents the uncompromising reality of his own personal experience: his own unwavering faithfulness to God through persecution and death, and his own resurrection and glorification beyond the grave. This he will share with all who are faithful to him, just as he offers the power which makes faithfulness possible. But in the moment of truth when persecution comes they must finally choose, and their choice is their judgement.

6

Heaven and the scroll with seven seals
(Rev 4:1–8:1)

The opening chapters of Revelation have established the audience for whom the whole book is written and the purpose of all the visions. The book is not written for the world at large, but for people who have already accepted the message of salvation preached by Christ's apostles. They are now the Christians, the baptised who are united to the risen and exalted Christ and acknowledge him as Lord of the universe.

In the narrow sense the book is addressed to the Christians of seven Churches in western Asia Minor, but what it has to say to them applies equally to Christian Churches wherever they may be. By this time – three generations after the crucifixion and resurrection of Jesus – Churches had been established throughout the eastern Roman Empire and further. With the destruction of Jerusalem in the Roman-Jewish War of 66-70 AD, the city could no longer be the administrative centre for Christians. The first Christians had all been Jews; by now most Christians were Gentiles.

Revelation reminds this wide Christian audience of the dangers of complacency. As the apostles had said in their preaching, Christ was sharing with them the glory of his resurrection and exultation, but this required their total commitment to him. The kind of response they gave to him would be the measure of their judgement. Persecution was spreading as Roman authorities began to understand what

Christians really claimed, and that would test the quality of their faith. Unimaginable glory awaited those who remained faithful to Christ, but failure would bring the kind of appalling judgement which John was about to witness in his visions.

The vision of God (4:1-11)

With the conclusion of the last of the letters which the risen and exalted Christ had dictated to him for the seven Churches under his charge, John's vision turned towards heaven. There he noticed that a door had opened, and the great voice of command which he heard at the beginning of his opening vision now spoke again. It told him to come through the door so that he could see what was about to happen to the universe.

It was a vision of God enthroned in the midst of his innermost group of courtiers, receiving their constant worship. The language used by John to describe what he saw is similar to the language used by the prophet Isaiah to describe his vision of God enthroned in the Temple (Is 6), and by the prophet Ezekiel to describe his vision of God in the Babylonian desert (Ezek 1 and 10).

Isaiah received his vision of God eight hundred years before John, at a crucial moment when the Assyrians were about to overrun Palestine and impose their will and their religion on the Hebrew people. Ezekiel received his vision, two hundred years after Isaiah, at one of the blackest periods in Hebrew history when there seemed no hope for God's people. Jerusalem and its Temple had been destroyed, and the flower of the Hebrew nation had been deported to Babylonia. Their visions reassured Isaiah and Ezekiel that God was still in control of events; he would rescue his people from their humiliation, punish their enemies and eventually lead them back to build a new Jerusalem.

John's vision of God enthroned and worshipped in heaven lays the same foundation for all that follows. John is imprisoned and his Churches are suffering persecution, but

God is enthroned and will impose his will on all powers, whether earthly or cosmic. Both God and his throne are bathed in glory like the light reflected by precious stones, and a crystal floor stretches out before it. Lightning flashes and rolls of thunder come from the divine throne, and seven flaming torches, which John says are the seven spirits of God, burn before it. The prophet Zechariah wrote of seeing seven lamps in a vision, which were 'the eyes of the Lord, which range through the whole earth' (Zech 4:10); the seven spirits of God are a further link between God and the world he rules.

Four living creatures flank the throne, each with six wings and a different face: a lion, an ox, a man and an eagle. John says that they are ceaselessly occupied in singing a hymn to God:

'Holy, holy, holy, is the Lord God Almighty, who was and is and is to come' (1:8).

John's description again echoes the language of Isaiah's and Ezekiel's visions (Is 6:2-3 and Ezek 1:5ff), evidence of their influence on John or of the authenticity of John's experience.

Surrounding God in John's vision are twenty-four enthroned elders, clothed in white and crowned with gold, like the associate judges seated round an emperor administering justice. Whenever the living creatures sang their hymn, the elders prostrated themselves before God's throne and sang a hymn of their own:

'Worthy art thou, our Lord and God,
to receive glory and honour and power,
for thou didst create all things,
and by thy will they existed and were created' (4:11).

The two hymns assert the eternal majesty of God, and the dependence of all things on his creative will for their very existence.

This perception of God is vitally important for all that follows. Nothing whatever in the universe, no matter how opposed to God it may try to be, is independent of him. It was brought into existence by God's will alone; it is sustained in every moment of its existence and in all it does by God alone; and God alone will determine its final fate. This applies equally to the evil forces as to the good ones. For John's Christians, the answer to the existence of evil and the damage it does must be sought in the nature of love; it cannot be explained away as a force with powers of its own.

A fundamental conclusion flows from this central truth of the Christian revelation. God's judgements about his creation and the consequences of those judgements are all moral ones, whether they are rewards or punishments. They are not mere expressions of power, in which God demonstrates his superiority over all other powers and his ability to do whatever he wishes. God's judgements are the consequences of what the creatures in his universe have done with the existence he has given them. Love is a pattern of free offer and free response, even God's love, and the consequences for creatures flow from the nature of their response to his love.

The scroll and the Lamb (5:1-14)

The heavenly drama in John's vision moves into a new phase when he sees that God is holding a rolled scroll fastened with seven seals. Breaking the first seal would give access to the opening section of the scroll, and successive sections could be read as the remaining seals were broken and the rest of the scroll was unrolled.

Like the decisions of a secular ruler, the scroll was a record of divine edicts, which did not become effective until they were published by unrolling the scroll. Only someone authorised by God could break the seals, and whoever did so would then be responsible for seeing that the orders contained in it – God's judgements on his creation – were carried out. It was a terrible responsibility, and the heavenly court could not find anyone in the whole creation who was worthy to open the scroll and implement its contents.

Then one of the elders told John that 'The Lion of the tribe of Judah, the Root of David' was worthy because he had conquered (6:5), and this person is immediately revealed as a lamb, marked with the wounds of sacrifice and having seven horns and eyes, standing next to God's throne. It is Christ, of course.

Two major images are used here to indicate his unique status. One is the messianic imagery derived from King David, the first king of the united Hebrew tribes and their liberator from the Philistines. David came from the tribe of Judah, which had been given the title of 'Lion' by the patriarch Jacob in his definitive blessing of his sons (Gen 49:9). The other image is even more powerful both for Christians and for Jews. It is that of the sacrificial lamb, first used of Christ by John the Baptist, and referring to the Passover lamb, sacrificed and eaten every year by all Jews to commemorate the escape from Egypt and all God's subsequent acts of salvation (Ex 12; Jn 1:29). The sanctified blood of the sacrificed lamb protected the worshippers from all evil and cleansed them from their sins. Applied to Jesus, it gathered into one symbol the significance of all he achieved by his life, death and resurrection.

Christ the Lamb, in John's vision, went to the throne and took the scroll from God. The heavenly court immediately worshipped the Lamb, and added the prayers of the 'saints' – all faithful Christians – as incense. Then they sang a new hymn to Christ to mark his new responsibilities as administrator of God's justice:

> 'Worthy art thou to take the scroll
>   and to open its seals,
> for thou wast slain
>   and by thy blood didst ransom men for God
> from every tribe and tongue

>   and people and nation,
> and hast made them a kingdom
>   and priests to our God,
> and they shall reign on earth' (6:9-10).

There are echoes here of the great covenant God made with the Hebrew people at Mount Sinai, the foundation of the Hebrew nation as God's special people, 'a kingdom of priests and a holy nation' (Ex 19:6). John hears the heavenly court proclaim that Christ had fulfilled this promise and inaugurated the new covenant, and the hymn is then taken up by the whole creation.

The first six seals (6:1-17)

One by one, the Lamb begins to open the seals of the scroll, and God's edicts recorded in the scroll immediately take effect. Six out of the seven seals release a different disaster for the earth and its inhabitants, and the other seal gives protection to those who have suffered persecution.

The descriptions are horrific, but the dynamic driving the imagery is the sense of outrage in the face of innocent suffering and persecution. John's people could only endure whatever persecutions were committed against them, just as Christ refused to counter his sufferings with violence. But they also believed that the universe was created and ruled by a just and all-powerful God, who would administer justice and redress all wrongs. The descriptions of disaster are a vivid expression of this confidence in the only imagery available to them.

The seven seals and the immediate consequences of breaking them are a summary of the events described in more detail in the rest of Revelation. Although set in the future, they also account for past disasters which have swept through human history. The Hebrew prophets repeatedly explained wars, famines and the rise and fall of military empires as God's punishment for national sins: 'They have sown the wind, and they shall reap the whirlwind' (Hos 8:7). The faithful also suffer, but they are brought safely through them by God to share his victory and to be the nucleus of a new start. So too in John's visions. The faithful are marked by God for survival and glory, but their persecutors and those who fail God when they are under pressure are destroyed horrifically.

The opening of the first four seals released four horsemen, the famous 'Horsemen of the Apocalypse', white, red, black and pale green, who each initiated a different disaster. The first rider carried a bow and wore a crown, symbolising an invincible conqueror. The second one had a huge sword and destroyed the earth's peacefulness, so that war and bloodshed broke out. The third carried scales for weighing rations, and symbolised famine and extortionate prices; only olive oil and wine are mysteriously exempted. The fourth rider is named Death, and is followed by Hades, the Lord of the Underworld in Greek mythology; their powers are increased beyond normal mortality rates, so that a quarter of earth's inhabitants die of violence, famine, disease and the attacks of wild animals.

They are familiar images of sudden disaster, reminiscent of the unexpected appearance of the ruthless horsemen who were the first signs of a devastating invasion. The disasters of the past and present are only the first signs of the final disasters which will express God's justice and restore his universal rule.

The disasters will be universal but those who are faithful to God will survive them. The opening of the fifth seal by the sacrificed Lamb gives an indication of this. It reveals the souls of the faithful who have already died under persecution 'for the word of God and for the witness they have borne' (6:9). In the opening passage of John's Gospel 'the Word of God' is Jesus himself, the living revelation of God's will and of the pattern of love. Jesus remained uncompromisingly faithful to that pattern of life even when it led to his death. So also with all those who died under persecution in the past, in the present when John's own people were being killed, and in the future; they like Jesus were witnesses revealing something about God.

The martyrs in John's vision were resting beneath the altar like the animals after sacrifices, and they called out to God and asked how long it would be before he judged those who killed them. They were given white robes and told that they must wait until all the martyrdoms yet to come on earth were finished, a warning to John's readers that there would be no immediate end of their sufferings.

The Lamb opened the sixth seal and the action had consequences which reversed the process of creation described at the opening of Genesis. The sun and moon were darkened, the stars fell, the sky rolled away and the earth was flattened. Such a display of power terrified even the mightiest of earth's rulers, and they called on the rocks to kill them so that they could escape 'the wrath of the Lamb' (6:16). Whatever impressions their past conquests may have generated, their power was only an illusion which God had now shattered.

The 144,000 (7:1-8)

For a brief period the sequence of disasters or the summaries of the disasters to come was suspended in John's vision, as God took steps to identify those who had been faithful to him and to protect them from what was to come. Four angels restrained the gales of destruction while a fifth angel came with God's seal.

Centuries before John, the prophet Ezekiel had recorded his vision of God protecting and avenging the exiled Hebrews in Babylonia. Ezekiel described an angel sent by God with writing implements to mark the foreheads of everyone who condemned idolatrous worship in Jerusalem; they were spared when God ordered the idolaters to be killed.

Similarly, the angel with God's seal in John's vision is told to mark the foreheads of 144,000 from the tribes of Israel, 12,000 from each tribe. It is only a selection from the total membership, signifying that only a fraction has been chosen for their faithfulness. Just as Ezekiel had seen God choose only faithful Hebrews for salvation, so now John's Christians could draw the same conclusion for themselves.

There is also an additional element of selection, which could easily be overlooked; one of the Hebrew tribes, Dan, does not appear in John's list, but there are still twelve tribes because John includes Levi, omitted from Hebrew lists because the Levites were priests without land. Some Hebrew traditions accused Dannites of being idolatrous (Judg 18; 1 Kgs 12:28-30), and there was even a tradition that Satan led them.

Later in Revelation it emerges that the 144,000 were the first human beings to be redeemed. They were specially chosen to accompany the Lamb on Mount Zion, and to sing a hymn of praise, known only to them (14:1-5). The prophet Isaiah had been the first to formulate clear teaching about a faithful 'remnant' who would form the nucleus of a new chosen people (Is 10:20-22). Isaiah had seen kings, priests and the educated classes of Jerusalem all betray their responsibilities and behave as if their inherited power guaranteed them the favour of God.

Revelation brings that ancient prophetic tradition to its fulfilment. God's purpose for his creation cannot be thwarted, and the final remnant who have remained faithful through persecution are to be forever with Christ at the centre of the new Jerusalem. John draws on the familiar, ancient Hebrew symbols to express the final hope he envisages for his Christian faithful.

The triumph of the elect (7:9-17)

The 144,000 are not the only members of humanity to join in the triumph and glory of the Lamb. John next says that he saw a countless crowd, composed of people from every human nation and ethnic group, clothed in white and carrying palm branches. Palm branches had long been carried by victorious armies as a sign of victory; they were (and still are) an important feature of the Hebrew Feast of Tabernacles to express rejoicing that the harvest has been safely gathered (Lev 23:40); and they had (and have) special significance for Christians because the crowd greeted Jesus with palm branches at his final entry into Jerusalem (Jn 12:13).

The great crowd stood with the Lamb before God's throne, says John, and sang a hymn of thanksgiving which acknowledged God as the source of their salvation. The other creatures attending the throne prostrated in worship, assented to the crowd's praise and added their own hymn praising seven attributes of God: 'Blessing and glory and wisdom and thanksgiving and honour and power and might be to our God for ever and ever!' (7:12).

Earlier in Revelation the heavenly court had cried that the Lamb was worthy to receive an almost identical list of gifts (5:12). Now all the inhabitants of heaven joined in a hymn praising God as the source of these gifts. Unlike the earlier list, each of the attributes in this later list is preceded by the definite article: 'the blessing and the glory and the wisdom...' The distinction between the two lists emphasises that God alone is the single uncreated and unbegotten source of all authority, however difficult it may be to put this into words.

In John's account, one of the elders attracted his attention to ask him a rhetorical question, 'Who are these, clothed in white robes, and whence have they come?' (7:13). John's answer implied that he did not know but that the elder could tell him. The elder went on to answer his own question: 'These are they who have come out of the great tribulation; they have washed their robes and made them white in the blood of the Lamb,' (7:14).

This literary structure serves to emphasise the importance of the elder's explanation for John's Christian readers. The great crowd is composed of all those who have been subjected to great trials during their lives on earth. John had just commented on the cosmopolitan nature of the crowd, drawn from the whole range of earth's inhabitants. So John's

Christian martyrs might be the centre of it, but anyone who has suffered at the hands of evil without submitting is included.

The reference to white robes washed in the blood of the Lamb would have made immediate sense to John's Christians. The imagery is drawn from two religious practices which would have been familiar to them, one from the rite of baptism and one from sacrificial ritual.

We should remember that Christians in John's time, towards the end of the first century, were baptised by total immersion and were given a white garment to wear as they left the water. This not only symbolised their cleansing from sins; it was also a sign of their union with the risen and exalted Christ. They had 'put on' Christ (Gal 3:27), and from then onwards all divisions of nationality, sex or social standing counted for nothing. They had entered into a new way of life shared with them by Christ.

This is combined here in Revelation with another everyday experience which is no longer commonly practised, that of animal sacrifice. In this religious rite, particularly for Hebrews, the blood had a special significance. As the seat of life, which came from God, the blood of the dedicated and sanctified animal was imbued with the creative and cleansing power of God. Wherever it was poured out, the blood increased the sanctity of that place, and the worshippers were cleansed from all ungodly defilement by being splashed with the sacrificial blood.

Jesus Christ's death was (and is) interpreted as a sacrifice by Christians, indeed as the ultimate sacrifice which rendered it unnecessary ever to sacrifice again. His blood shed at his crucifixion was the releasing of the final, apocalyptic power to cleanse. As an interim measure until the final consummation of God's plans for his creation, the Christian Eucharist or 'Lord's Supper' gives access to this power: 'Drink of it, all of you; for this is my blood of the new covenant, which is poured out for many for the forgiveness of sins,' (Mt 26:27-28). But John is describing the final stages, when all those who have been cleansed by Christ's sacrifice join him round the throne of God. They have washed their robes in the blood of the Lamb.

The blessed are now spending their whole being in the worship of God. There is no temple in heaven because the presence of God enthroned turns the whole heavenly existence into a temple, so the elder can say that they serve God day and night within his temple (8:15):

'They shall hunger no more,
    neither thirst any more;
the sun shall not strike them,
    nor any scorching heat.
For the Lamb in the midst of the throne
    will be their shepherd,
and he will guide them
    to springs of living water;
and God shall wipe away
    every tear from their eyes' (8:16-17).

It is hardly surprising that this passage is so often read at funerals. It sums up the Christian hope of salvation in the kind of simple imagery which everyone can appreciate, which echoes similar imagery in such psalms as 'The Lord is my shepherd' (Ps 23). But the context of the passage in Revelation also shows starkly that Christians cannot afford to be complacent about this as their destiny. If the images of salvation are attractive, the images of damnation which surround them in Revelation are utterly repellent. Neither set of images is a literal description, but both sets point into an equally certain reality.

The seventh seal (8:1)

The events following the opening of the first six seals of the scroll are like a preview of what is to follow. The final stages of God's plan could not be set in train until the life, death and resurrection of Jesus the Christ. With Christ's ascension to glory he is at God's side to administer the divine edicts of judgement which will round off the history of the universe, just as he was at God's side at the beginning to administer the divine edicts of creation.

The crucified Lamb, image of humility and submission, is also the judge. Christ has offered all humanity the fullest possible share in his own power and in his victory over evil. Now it is time for him to evaluate humanity's response to his offer; to reward beyond their imagination all who have responded, who have been able to share his own humility and submission to suffering; and to express God's final rejection of those who have failed to respond.

Six seals have been opened so far. The opening of the seventh seal initiates the full and final conflict which marks the end of the universe. The immediate effect of opening the last seal is an immense silence in heaven. In terms of the dramatic structure and development of John's visions, the silence at this critical moment heightens the drama like the proverbial calm before a storm or a lull before the final onslaught in a terrible battle.

But a deeper significance may legitimately be read into this particular silence. All of the great theologians have found themselves driven into silence by the realisation that it is impossible to find adequate words and images for the profound truths they are trying to describe. Real contact with God induces above all a deep sense of awe, the biblical experience sometimes translated misleadingly as fear.

As the moment is reached when the world's history reaches its climax in God's final judgement, a silence descends on the whole of heaven; for this is also the final revelation of the moral truth by which all history is judged, and of God's power to execute justice. The silence is more telling than the terrible images that follow it.

7

The seven trumpets
(Rev 8:2–11:19)

As John's visions move into the final stages of the last judgement, the significance of the new development is underlined by an echo of the earlier moment when the Lamb first unsealed the great scroll. Then also there had been a period of silence, even though that silence differed because it sprang from the frustration and fear that no one was worthy to break the seals (5:2-4). Then also the decisive event was preceded by golden censers from which the incense rising to the throne of God represented the prayers of the saints (5:8).

When the Lamb opened the final, seventh seal of the great scroll, John reports that there was first a long silence in heaven, not of frustration this time but of anticipation and awe. Then he saw seven trumpets being given to the seven angels who stood before God. These angels are closely associated with the seven spirits of God, the seven stars held by Christ which symbolised the angels of John's seven Churches, and the seven lampstands with their flaming torches which were the Churches themselves (1:12-20).

The prayers of the saints (8:2-5)

The linkage is important because it associates the members of the Churches with the judgement of the universe. Before the seven angels sounded their trumpets another angel appeared with a golden censer; he was given a great quantity of incense which he mixed with the prayers of the 'saints' and then offered to God on the golden altar which stood before his throne. The incense and the prayers rose before God like petitions presented to a king. Consequently, all that now follows may be seen as the granting by God of the petitions of the churches. The 'saints' are those Christians who have proved their holiness by remaining faithful to God during persecution, and God now associates them with his actions as he brings judgement on those who have opposed him.

This is underlined by the climax of the angel's offering of the incense and prayers. As the smoke rose before God, the angel filled the censer again with burning coals from the altar and threw it down to the earth, where it caused great storms and an earthquake. These were merely the preliminary warnings of the punishments that were to follow, but they were the immediate and direct result of the anguished prayers of the faithful pleading for justice as they endured their persecution. John's thoughts on the prison island of Patmos were never far from his persecuted Churches on the nearby mainland and the practical comfort they would find in his descriptions of his visions.

The first four trumpets (8:6-13)

John's account of his visions is permeated by the number seven: seven Churches, seven angels who are God's guardians of the Churches and his messengers to them; seven seals fastening the great scroll; and now, seven trumpets. In ancient numerology, seven represents completion, the sum of the sides of a square and a triangle, the two basic geometrical figures which between them symbolise the cosmos of heaven and earth.

The plagues and disasters which followed the breaking of each of the seven seals were particularly directed at the human inhabitants of the world who ignored or defied God, and had filled history with violence, oppression and the persecution of God's faithful. But even here the punishment of the guilty was only a limited one. The time had now come in the unfolding drama of judgement for the process to be completed and for it to be extended to the whole of the universe. This indicates that the whole creation is under the direct control of God. The universe, God's creation, is a single entity and the history of every part of it affects the history of the rest of the creation.

Such a view is firmly rooted in the accounts of the creation of the universe in the opening chapters of the Book of Genesis. The way in which God created everything that exists is depicted there as a systematic and ordered process. Mankind is part of the creation, and also the administrator of it. Made in God's image and knowing God's mind, mankind is given the responsibility for regulating the earth in accordance with God's overall plan for every aspect of it, so that each part of the creation can make its appropriate contribution to the perfection of the whole of it.

Our own times are realising afresh that humanity and the rest of creation are integral parts of one whole, inseparable from each other and affecting each other. Our attempts to be independent of God rebound on the whole of creation and distort it in every aspect. John's vision of the final consequences reflects this insight as the angels sound the trumpets of judgement.

The first trumpet call produced a storm of hail, fire and blood which fell on the earth and destroyed a third of the land and its vegetation; this is an echo of the seventh plague of Egypt, which also destroyed all vegetation by a rain of hail, fire and blood except in the part of Egypt where the Hebrews lived (Ex 9:22-26). So there is an element of selective salvation even in this image of destruction. At the second trumpet call a volcano erupted in the sea.

The waters turned to blood and destroyed a third of the ships and sea-creatures. Once again there is an echo of one of the plagues of Egypt, when the River Nile was turned to blood and became undrinkable (Ex 7:17-21).

At the third trumpet call a blazing star fell to earth and turned a third of the rivers and springs of water to wormwood, which made the water bitter and poisonous. Wormwood as a herb yielding a bitter oil is a biblical symbol for Hebrew idolaters who spread through the nation like a poison (Deut 29:18). In his condemnation of such Hebrews who deserted God for pagan worship, Jeremiah wrote that God would punish them with wormwood:

> 'Thus says the Lord of hosts, the God of Israel: Behold, I will feed this people with wormwood, and give them poisonous water to drink. I will scatter them among the nations whom neither they nor their fathers have known; and I will send the sword after them, until I have consumed them' (Jer 9:15-16).

For Jeremiah, wormwood was a symbol of punishment by exile, humiliation and persecution. In John's vision of the final judgement, it is a symbol for the kind of death awaiting those who turned to other gods.

At the fourth trumpet call a third part of the sun, moon and stars was destroyed, so that their light was dimmed. In the first account of creation, at the beginning of the Book of Genesis, the planets and stars not only provide light for mankind and earth's creatures; they also mark the passage of the seasons, they indicate the proper times for the various activities of the agricultural year, and they tell mankind when to celebrate the religious festivals. Disrupting them as an act of judgement throws all mankind's normal routines into confusion.

The fifth and sixth trumpets: locusts and plagues (9:1-21)

In the beliefs of the ancient world the stars were personal spiritual powers for good or evil; such beliefs survive today in the popular interest in astrology. Orthodox Judaism and Christianity both took such beliefs for granted, but insisted that all such powers – however great – were only subordinate to the one God, who used them as messengers or servants.

The sounding of the fifth trumpet was the signal in John's visions for another star to fall from heaven to earth holding the key to the shaft leading to the abyss. Both Greeks and Romans believed that the dead went to this region beneath the earth, which was not a place of punishment. Mainstream Judaism, which did not believe in the resurrection of the body, had a similar belief in an underworld, 'Sheol', where the dead went to a shadowy existence of utter inactivity. King Saul persuaded a medium to bring the prophet Samuel back from Sheol to tell him the future, and Samuel asked him why he had disturbed him by bringing him up (1 Sam 28:8-19).

Hebrew beliefs about the underworld slowly changed from Sheol as a place of eternal rest to Sheol as a vast grave with many areas in it where the dead exist in various states depending on the kind of lives they had lived while on earth. By the time John recorded his apocalyptic visions the underworld had become an abyss of horrors, from which only God could deliver. Jesus promised that its powers would never overcome his Church (Mt 16:18), and at the beginning of the Book of Revelation the risen Christ carries the keys of death and the abyss.

The angelic star sent from heaven at the fifth trumpet call with the key to the abyss now opened it, and a great column of smoke rose from it in John's vision. Locusts crowned with gold and as large as armoured horses emerged from the smoke; they had human faces, lions' teeth and tails of scorpions' stings. Led by 'the angel of the bottomless pit' named Abaddon, they fanned out through the earth with power to sting all who did not have God's seal on their foreheads. 'Abaddon' is the Hebrew for 'destruction', so the name designates the angel of destruction. Earlier, John had described seeing an angel mark God's servants with a seal to protect them from the approaching terrors (7:3-8).

Terrible though they were, the stings of the scorpion locusts did not kill, says John, but the pain was so intense that those who had been stung longed to die. Again there is an echo of the plagues of Egypt, when locusts were sent to bring a season of suffering by destroying all the crops and fruit trees but not to kill the people themselves (Ex 10:3-20).

At the sixth trumpet call John heard a voice from the horns of the golden altar before the throne of God. Horns were a symbol of power, so this voice spoke with the direct authority of God as it ordered the angel of the sixth trumpet to release the four angels who were held in restraint at the banks of the River Euphrates. This was one of the four rivers flowing from the Garden of Eden (Gen 2:14), but it was also the heartland of the great Mesopotamian empires which controlled the destinies of the Hebrew people through most of their history. In particular, the Babylonians had exiled the survivors of Jerusalem to the banks of the Euphrates after they had destroyed the city six centuries before Christ.

In John's vision, the four angels of the Euphrates rode out through the earth at the head of an army numbering millions mounted on horses with lions' heads breathing out fire, smoke and sulphur, whose tails were venomous snakes. This vast host spread plague wherever it went, which killed a further third of mankind, but John says that the survivors only continued in their idolatrous worship, their witchcraft and their violent crimes.

The appalling punishments depicted in these visions of the attacks by God on mankind are a measure of God's power and of his universal jurisdiction. But running through it all like a thread is the opportunity to turn from the activities which offend God, to repent and be numbered among the saved. The punishments are warnings as well as retributions, but they go unheeded. So the punishment continues, ever more terrible as God unleashes further dimensions of his power.

The small scroll and the two witnesses (10:1-11:14)

At this point John's vision of an unfolding sequence of cosmic punishments was interrupted. A further mighty angel descended from heaven to earth carrying a small, open scroll. The angel was clothed in a cloud with his head surrounded by a rainbow halo; his face was as bright as the sun, says John, and his legs like pillars of fire. He straddled the sea and land and the voice with which he made his proclamation was like the sound of seven thunders. John says that he was about to record the angel's words when a voice from heaven forbade him to do so. The Book of Daniel records a similar incident and a similar prohibition when the prophet was forbidden to reveal words which were 'shut up and sealed until the end of time' (Dan 12:6-13). Although that time was clearly very near in John's visions, it had not yet arrived and its secrets would not be revealed until the seventh trumpet call.

John says that he was then commanded to take the small scroll from the angel and eat it; he would find it would taste sweet but be bitter after he had swallowed it. This is an exact repetition of the command received by the prophet Ezekiel to eat a scroll (Ezek 2:8–3:3). The sweetness represents the desirability of God's words of command, but the bitterness in this case indicates the terrible consequences of them.

The 'word' of God is a familiar feature of the prophetic writings and preaching, where it refers to God's commands which are bound to be effective once the prophet has spoken them. John now becomes an active participant in the events of his visions, rather than a mere observer and recorder, for he says that he was told to 'prophesy about many peoples and nations and tongues and kings' (10:11). Like the Hebrew prophets, he has become a herald of God's decisions, which take effect as soon as his appointed servants make them known. It is a powerful assertion that apostles like John are heralds of judgement as well as messengers of salvation.

With further echoes of Ezekiel, John says that he was then given a surveyor's measuring staff and told to measure out the limits of the innermost sanctuary with its altar and worshippers, but not to measure the outer courts. This mysterious command takes its significance from the design of the great Hebrew Temple in Jerusalem, which consisted of an area containing the temple building and the altar of burnt offerings, surrounded by a series of courtyards. Only the Hebrew priests could enter the innermost area, while the series of courtyards provided carefully graded access for Hebrew men, women and Gentiles.

The limits imposed on John indicate that the great multitude of the faithful admitted to the innermost area of worship in heaven constitute a new priesthood. Such a promise was made by God to the Hebrew people at the Mount Sinai covenant, immediately after the exodus from Egypt – that they would be 'a kingdom of priests' (Ex 19:6). This promise was applied by Christians to the new covenant inaugurated by the death and resurrection of Christ, that they were 'a chosen race, a royal priesthood, a holy nation, God's own people' (1 Pet 2:9). Clearly, John believed that this promise was to be fulfilled for the members of his persecuted Churches who remained faithful to God during their sufferings.

John was next promised that 'two witnesses' would also be given power to prophesy, and so to deliver judgement in the name of God. With echoes again of the plagues of Egypt, these two witnesses would bring drought, turn water to blood and cause plagues. Then the beast from the abyss would attack the two witnesses and kill them. All who had been punished by them would at first gloat over their bodies, but God would raise them from the dead and take them to heaven in the sight of all their enemies. There would be a great earthquake which would kill many and lead many to repent.

The imagery of prophecy, death, resurrection and ascension closely follows the pattern of Christ's earthly ministry, his crucifixion, and his vindication by the Father in resurrection and ascension. New Testament Christianity held that a similar pattern would also be experienced by those who were faithful followers of Christ, and particularly by the apostles.

The 'two witnesses' are further described as olive trees in John's vision, following the similar vision described by the

Old Testament prophet Zechariah. Writing immediately after the return of the surviving Hebrews from the Babylonian exile, Zechariah referred to the two Hebrew leaders, Joshua and Zerubbabel, as two olive trees pouring out oil. Consecrated olive oil was the material used for the ceremonial anointing of priests and kings to indicate that they were empowered by God to act in his name. Describing the two martyred witnesses as olive trees in John's vision would associate them closely with the persecuted Christians of John's Churches and with their imprisoned pastor.

The seventh trumpet (11:15-19)

As might be expected from the final event of a series of seven, the seventh trumpet call marks the beginning of a new phase in the final stages of the history of the universe. John says that immediately following it he heard a voice proclaiming that the kingdom of the world had become the kingdom of our Lord and of his Christ, and that he would reign for ever and ever (11:15).

The ascension of Jesus Christ forty days after his resurrection from the dead was not merely the end of his work amongst his disciples on earth; it marked the beginning of his reign as Lord of the universe, which included all the secular organisations on earth. History from then onwards would be a time for implementing Christ's victory over evil and death, and extending it throughout the earth and the ages. The method would still be the same: God's initiative of love inviting mankind's response, but there could no longer be any doubt about the outcome whatever setbacks there might still seem to be.

John's vision of the proclamation of Christ's kingdom is the final culmination of the process which – in terms of earthly events – began with the conception and birth of Jesus, or even with Jesus' 'emptying of himself' of his divine glory before his birth, referred to by Paul (Phil 2:4).

This latest development in John's visions is also a reminder of the ultimate reality revealed when heaven was first opened to him, God enthroned in glory with the twenty-four elders falling before him in worship. This time John saw them praising God for demonstrating his eternal power in judgement of the great earthly rulers:

'The nations raged, but thy wrath came,
and the time for the dead to be judged,
for rewarding thy servants, the prophets and saints,
and those who fear thy name, both small and great,
and for destroying the destroyers of the earth' (11:18).

Yet more of the architecture of heaven was revealed as the heavenly temple opened again so that the Ark of the Covenant could be seen in the innermost sanctuary. The symbolism of this ultimate revelation of the secrets of God's temple is derived from the Hebrew Temple in Jerusalem, where the Ark of the Covenant had been stored in an innermost sanctuary which only the high priest could enter. The ark itself, a portable shrine, was the visible symbol of God's protective presence, first constructed at Mount Sinai and carried before the people during their journey through the wilderness from Egypt to the Promised Land. It was destroyed along with the first Temple when the Babylonians destroyed Jerusalem in 587 BC, but it remained the most potent symbol in the Hebrew religion.

The heavenly temple had been opened before in John's visions (15:5), but only to release the seven angels with the seven bowls of plague. Now the work of that series of plagues and of the series following the trumpet calls had been completed, and the secrets of the temple could be revealed as their culmination rather than their beginning. John says that the revelation was accompanied by lightning, thunder, earth tremors and hail, echoing the phenomena which accompanied the revelations and the covenant at Mount Sinai (Ex 19). This completes the first cycle of visions, which began with the first visions of Christ's judgement of the seven Churches under John's jurisdiction. The visions moved on to reveal the heavenly worship of God enthroned in power and glory. This divine power was expressed in judgement of the universe and of all mankind initiated by the unsealing of the great scroll and the sounding of the seven trumpets.

The great multitude of those who had remained faithful were seen joining in the worship of God and of the risen Christ in heaven, but those who had defied God and persecuted his people were punished and destroyed by appalling plagues. God had been revealed as Lord of the entire universe: heaven, earth and the underworld, and of all its inhabitants whether human, angelic or monstrous. All were shown to be God's creatures and subject to his will. Moreover, the process of history itself was under the direct control of God, who would use it as an instrument of his justice to reveal his invincible righteousness.

In some ways, the second cycle of visions, from 12:1 to 22:5, is a repetition of the revelations of the first cycle in a different form.

8

The woman, the dragon and the beasts
(Rev 12:1–13:18)

The pregnant woman and the dragon

One of the best known passages in the Book of Revelation occurs at the beginning of Chapter 12 and marks the start of the second cycle of John's visions. It is the vision of a woman clothed with the sun and wearing a crown of twelve stars; her feet rest on the moon. She is pregnant and is crying out with the start of her labour pains. Of all the vivid apocalyptic scenes, this has been the one most frequently chosen by artists as the subject of paintings – even if they have not laid much emphasis on the woman's labour pangs.

In John's vision, the woman is not alone, for a red dragon appears, with seven crowned heads and ten horns, and removes a third of the stars from heaven with a sweep of its great tail. The dragon then stands before the woman, waiting to snatch her child and eat it as soon as it is born.

The woman gives birth to a boy destined to rule all nations, but before the dragon can snatch the child he is taken up to God's throne. His mother flees to a place of safety prepared for her in the desert, where she is fed for 1,260 days.

There are two main routes for the interpretation of this vision, and the two routes eventually coalesce and lead to the same truths. The first starts from the story of the Fall in the Book of Genesis (Gen 3), where the serpent tempts Eve, the first woman, to eat some of the fruit of the Tree of the

Knowledge of Good and Evil, which God had forbidden. After she had eaten, she gave some to Adam her husband, the first man, and he also ate.

According to Genesis, all the evils of the world stem from this first act of disobedience: the openness and trust between man and wife was damaged; enmity and murder developed between Adam and Eve's children; and mankind's harmony with nature was broken.

Within Hebrew tradition and other neighbouring cultures, this tree represented the power to control everything that had been created, and to decide what was good for it and what was evil. Under God's guidance or 'knowledge', everything in the creation had its proper place in God's plan and found its fulfilment there. When Adam and Eve ate the fruit they were asserting the right to organise the creation for their own selfish ends without reference to God. This was mankind believing the serpent's words, 'You will be like God' (Gen 3:5).

Only God could undo this universal damage, and he did so by sending his Son Jesus Christ into the world to restore the original harmony and so bring the world back to God again. Mary accepted God's invitation to be mother of Jesus, and by doing so she undid Eve's original act of disobedience. Mary's obedience made the birth of Jesus possible, and started the process of redemption. Consequently, the woman clothed with the sun in John's vision represents Mary, pregnant with Jesus. The dragon is the serpent, grown huge with evil power, waiting to destroy Jesus as soon as he is born. But God rescues both Mary and Jesus; Jesus is to be heavenly Lord of the universe restoring God's harmony; Mary is to follow him later after experiencing a full lifetime of deprivation during which she is protected by God from the serpent's sin.

The second route for interpretation passes through the history of the Hebrew people. God chose this nation, made his covenant with them and gave them the holy law to live by. This was so that they could be a centre of obedience, worship and divine harmony, where all mankind could find God and discover the peace and fulfilment God had always intended for his creation.

One of the most powerful images in this interpretation represents the Hebrew nation, Israel, as God's bride:

> 'Your Maker is your husband,
> the Lord of hosts is his name;
> and the Holy One of Israel is your redeemer,
> the God of the whole earth he is called.
> For the Lord has called you
> like a wife forsaken and grieved in spirit,
> like a wife of youth...
> With everlasting love
> I will have compassion on you' (Is 54:5-8).

Eventually, the Messiah will be the fruit of this marriage between God and his chosen people.

The Hebrew people suffered conquest, and even exiles, under a succession of international powers in the course of their history, but they survived. The prophets saw this as evidence of God's protection and they sometimes depicted the conquering empires as horned beasts which threatened God's people and could even destroy the stars (Dan 7:7; 8:9-12). God eventually sent a messianic figure to destroy the beasts and impose his rule over his creation, but the damage the battle caused symbolised the sufferings of Israel, God's bride.

This route again leads to Mary and Jesus, for Mary was also the representative of the Hebrew people when God invited her to be mother of his Son. John's vision contains the prophetic imagery of the forces of evil as a horned beast, but it is unable to destroy Mary or her newly born child. The sufferings of the woman clothed with the sun, including her exile under God's protection in the wilderness, sum up Hebrew history, but God was about to send his own forces in John's vision, to defeat the evil of the dragon.

The heavenly war (12:7-17)

The next dramatic development in John's vision of events in heaven at the end of time is the outbreak of a full-scale battle between God's angelic forces led by the archangel Michael, and the angelic forces of the dragon. God's forces win this battle and expel the dragon and its evil forces from heaven to earth. John identifies the dragon as 'the ancient serpent, who is called the Devil and Satan (12:9).

There can be no doubt that 'the ancient serpent' as a title refers to the snake which successfully tempted Eve to disobey God in the Garden of Eden (Gen 3:1-6). In that primitive explanation of the origins of all the evils in the creation, the serpent's attack on Eve's integrity set in train the ever-widening circles of disobedience, disorder and sin. John's vision echoes and develops the symbolism of the Garden of Eden, but this time the woman is protected by God against the serpent – now revealed as explicitly evil – and successfully evades its attacks.

The title 'Satan' needs to be treated with caution because there is a clear development in the meaning of the title within the Bible itself. Early occurrences of the name only apply it to an 'adversary', such as a prosecuting lawyer who helps a court to arrive at the truth (1 Chron 21:1; Job 1-2). At this stage Satan is one of God's angelic officials who helps to evaluate the integrity and strength of God's servants, such as King David and Job, by subjecting them to tests with God's approval.

In the four Gospels this meaning may still be seen in the temptations of Jesus by 'Satan' (Mk 1:13); and Jesus' rebuke of Peter as 'Satan' when he tried to dissuade Jesus from going to Jerusalem (Mt 16:23). But the conflation of 'Satan' and 'the Devil' is also there in the Gospels. The accounts of the temptations of Jesus use 'Devil' as an alternative title for Satan (Lk 4:2,10). Jesus speaks of 'Satan's kingdom' being divided against itself, where this is clearly a regime opposed to God (Mt 12:26). John's Gospel says that 'the Devil had already put it into the heart of Judas Iscariot' to betray Jesus;

then 'Satan' enters into Judas Iscariot and Jesus tells him to go and do it quickly (Jn 13:2,27).

Belief in a devil who leads the demonic forces was widespread amongst the people of the Middle East, and the Jewish and Christian traditions recorded in the Bible took this for granted. It fits the human experience of manifold evil in a world opposed to God, which is greater than mere human evil yet deeply influences human behaviour. Consequently, mere human effort cannot overcome or escape such evil, but needs delivering from it by a greater power.

But there is a vitally important difference between the Jewish and Christian beliefs on the one hand, and the beliefs of religious traditions where the forces of evil are independent of the good gods and equal in power to them. For Jews and Christians there is never any question of the Devil being equal to God in any way. He is God's creature and his power is subordinate to God's power. However disobedient the Devil and his evil forces may be, God's power is infinitely superior and will defeat and destroy evil at the appropriate time. John's visions depict the events of that time as God's final triumph and destruction of all evil and disobedience in his creation; hence the hymn which follows the heavenly defeat of the dragon in the visions:

> 'Now the salvation and the power
> and the kingdom of our God
> and the authority of his Christ
> have come...' (12:10).

The victory, however, had yet to be extended to the earth, and meanwhile in John's vision the dragon is able to attack the woman. This is not a new attack, but another description of the attack earlier described by John (12:6). To enable her to escape, the woman is given eagle's wings by God, as if in fulfilment of Isaiah's prophecy that they who wait for the Lord shall renew their strength and mount up with wings like eagles (Is 40:31). She escapes to the desert sanctuary God had prepared for her, where she is protected for one of those mysterious periods – 'a time, and times, and half a time' – for which there is no clear interpretation.

Like the sea monster which symbolised uncontrollable evil for the Hebrews, the dragon then produces a river in spate from its mouth to overwhelm the woman, but the earth produces a chasm which swallows the river before it can reach her. Frustrated, the dragon turns on the woman's offspring, 'those who keep the commandments of God and bear testimony to Jesus' (12:17). This is the clearest indication that the woman in the visions also represents the Church, whose faithful members must continue to expect persecution even though the final victory over evil has already been won.

John's message for his flock is indeed one of hope, but John is realistic about their actual situation. As Paul explained in his Letters, particularly 2 Corinthians, Christ's cosmic victory over evil was won at the cost of his suffering, and his followers can expect to share his suffering as well as his victory.

The beast from the sea (13:1-10)

Immediately after the dragon had taken up its stance on the seashore of earth in John's vision, ready to begin its attack on members of mankind who have been faithful to God, the symbolism of a sea monster occurs again. This time it is not the dragon itself which is the monster but a seven-headed beast which emerges from the sea, each head crowned and horned to indicate its power to subjugate, and bearing a blasphemous name. It combines the physical features of a leopard, a bear and a lion. The dragon gives it power and authority, says John, and people worship it.

The obvious parallel for this beast is to be found in the Book of the prophet Daniel, where similar beasts are armed with horns to indicate their power to terrify the earth. There is little doubt that in Daniel the beasts symbolise the international empires which successively conquered the

Hebrew people. In Daniel they were defeated by the messianic Son of Man.

Here in John's vision, the beast most probably represents the power of the Roman Empire from the time of the Emperor Nero. The seven heads would be the sequence of Roman emperors up to Nero, who initiated the persecution of Christians following the great fire of Rome (AD 64) and executed Peter and Paul. Under Nero the worship of the Roman emperor as a god was taken seriously; where it was enforced Christians found themselves having to defy an imperial decree for the first time. The blasphemous name on the beast's heads would reflect the emperors' blasphemous claim to worship.

By the time of John's visions, Rome's power stretched from Britain in the west to Syria, and from the Black Sea to Egypt, an area sufficiently large and diverse to suggest that God had allowed Rome to have authority for a period 'over every tribe and people and tongue and nation' (13:7). Even the fact that in John's vision one of the beast's heads is wounded fits Nero; Nero committed suicide but there was widespread belief that being a god he would return from the dead to rule over Rome again.

As John himself and the people of his Churches were suffering persecution from the Romans, his vision of the beast from the sea would be particularly important. Its eventual defeat by God signified that their sufferings would culminate in glory.

The beast from the earth (13:11-18)

As John watched he says that he saw a second beast appear, this time from the earth. This one has only one head, which looked like a lamb with two horns, but it speaks with all the power of a dragon.

Again there are echoes here of the Book of Daniel, where the prophet reports seeing a two-horned ram which charged about destroying all in its path. In Daniel the ram represented the Persian empire, but the function of the lamb-like beast in John's vision is to be a propagandist for the beast from the sea. As its prophet it convinces the inhabitants of the earth to worship the first beast, and it supports its teaching with miracles, including fire brought down from heaven.

There are warnings in the Old Testament and in the New against 'false prophets'. In Deuteronomy, Moses warns the people that they must ignore any prophet who tells them that they should worship other gods, even if the prophet is able to support his teaching with miracles and dreams. Jesus himself warns his disciples against false teachers who will appear in the last days and support their teaching with miracles 'so as to lead astray, if possible, even the elect' (Mt 24:24). It is also clear from Paul's Letters that the early Christian communities were plagued with unorthodox itinerant teachers whose teachings contradicted those of the apostles (e.g. 2 Cor 11:12-15).

As false prophet, the beast in John's vision may represent a whole range of authorities: Jewish and Christian teachers who wrongly taught that emperor-worship was compatible with strict Jewish and Christian traditions; and Roman officials who similarly tried to get Christians to take part in the state worship along with their own distinctively Christian worship.

The beast in John's vision reinforces its authority by granting a monopoly of all commerce to those who had been stamped on their foreheads or their right hands with the name of the first beast 'or the number of its name' (13:17). This again reinforces the interpretation that associates both beasts with the Roman authorities, who regulated and taxed trade throughout the empire.

The beast's number, says John, is 666. This strange equation depends on the use of the letters of ancient alphabets as numbers (the familiar modern numerical system is derived at a much later date from the Arabs). Each letter was assigned a particular number, such as in the Roman system where $I = 1, V = 5, X = 10$, etc. The letters of a name could therefore also form a number, or their numerical equivalents be added together to give a number.

The Emperor Nero's title, 'Caesar Nero', consists of letters which can be combined to provide the number 666, so Nero is the main candidate for the beast of John's vision, and such a cryptic reference would protect the Christians who understood it and interpreted it. But the original interpretation amongst Christians in John's time and locality has been lost and there have been many suggestions of candidates other than Nero. The persecution of the first two or three generations of Christians by civil authorities was patchy and localised. Everything depended on the attitudes of the local Roman governor and the native magistrates, who were more concerned with keeping the peace and protecting vested interests than in enforcing general laws. That would be of little comfort to Christians in a district where they were suffering persecution for their beliefs, but it did mean that any of the emperors could be blamed for the acts of local administrators acting in his name. John was a bishop concerned with strengthening his own flock, and his images represent the forces of evil attacking his own people.

Both beasts can be seen as antichrists in their different ways. The first beast's return from death to impose its rule is a clear caricature of the resurrection of Jesus. It is also a warning against miracles as a proof of truth, for even resurrection from death can be misleading if it supports teaching which contradicts the love of God taught by Jesus and expressed by him in every moment and every encounter of his ministry. The second beast's similarity to a lamb is also an antichrist symbol derived from the Christian symbolism of Jesus as the 'Lamb of God' (Jn 1:29) which also occurs so frequently in John's visions (5:6 etc). There is little danger of any such misunderstanding within the structure of John's visions. Not only will the beasts be destroyed by God; before that and immediately following his description of their appearing from the sea and the earth, John contrasts them with a vision of Jesus as Lamb of God in heaven surrounded by his followers. However powerful the forces of evil may appear to be on earth to the people who are suffering, they cannot bear comparison with the heavenly reality of God's saving power.

9

The triumph of the Lamb over Babylon
(Rev 14:1–20:15)

As John's horrific visions moved towards their climax he was given further reassurances that the cataclysmic events he was witnessing were only aimed at those who oppose God. God's terrible power is also expressed in the gentleness of the Lamb, who is God's salvation for all who are faithful to God. But the destruction of God's enemies in these visions is comprehensive and total, whether the enemy is a power of heavenly magnitude threatening the whole universe or is only the nameless multitude who worship it.

At the end of the decisive battles comes the last judgement, when God completes his campaign with the final punishment of the forces of evil and the reward of all who have remained faithful to him. So far, the campaign has only involved the living; now all people who have died are called before God for judgement. It demonstrates that the whole of God's creation, from the beginning of time, must derive its values from God alone and must give account of themselves to God. However powerful or attractive other powers may have seemed, no beings at any time have really been independent of the God who created all things, nor could God permit them to give worship and allegiance to any other.

Three visions of reassurance (14:1-20)

The visions reassuring John of God's abiding power were given to him for the sake of his persecuted flock in Asia Minor, as well as for his own comfort. The first vision is again of the Lamb of God surrounded by the 144,000 who had earlier been sealed on their foreheads with God's name because they had proved that they were 'the servants of God' (7:4-8). The number symbolised the twelve tribes of the 'new' Israel, the followers of Christ who had inherited the covenant God had made with the people of the twelve tribes of Israel when he rescued them from their slavery in Egypt.

In the visions John had just received, the blasphemous beast which ruled the earth was surrounded by its followers, who had been sealed on their foreheads with the number of the beast (13:16). By contrast, the Lamb of God, whose sacrifice proves more powerful than the beast and its powers, is here surrounded by his followers. The Lamb and his followers stand on Mount Zion, one of the names for the Temple Mount in Jerusalem, the only place on earth where the Jewish religion permitted the daily sacrifices which made God's saving power available to his chosen people.

There was now no further need for such sacrifices because Jesus, the Lamb of God, had given himself as the ultimate sacrifice. According to the prophets, Mount Zion was also the place where God would finally judge all peoples, the place where the Messiah would first appear and the place where the faithful would find safety during God's final battle against evil (e.g. Obad 17).

In John's vision, the 144,000 are praising the Lamb in secret words known only to themselves, and once again John thought it was like the sound of a great torrent of water, or continuous peals of thunder, permeated by the music of massed harps. John describes all the worshippers as virgins who had never been defiled with women; in the idioms used by John to express his visions, this description means that they had never taken part in pagan or idolatrous worship.

The Old Testament frequently describes such illicit worship in sexual terms because it was often associated with the sacral prostitutes of the pagan temples who provided sexual intercourse as a form of religious experience.

Fortunately, John makes it clear that the 144,000 are not the only members of the human race to be saved. As we have seen, the number is the symbolic description of the new Israel rather than the literally total number of people to be saved. But they are also only the 'first fruits' of God's harvest, representing all who will be gathered to God. In the old traditional Hebrew harvest festivals, the very first part of each crop was offered in sacrifice to sanctify the whole crop and acknowledge that it was God who had brought it to its full maturity.

John says that the vision of the Lamb and its companions was followed by a vision of three angels flying high above him and announcing messages to all humankind from God.

The first angel proclaims 'an eternal gospel', the everlasting good news that the time has come for God to sit in judgement. The good news was an invitation for all people to worship him as the only source of the whole creation,

> 'Worship him who made heaven and earth, the sea and the fountains of water' (14:7).

God's authority to judge is inseparable from his power as the sole creator and sustainer of all that exists. The whole creation is designed by him to reflect his values, so God's judgement of all peoples will be determined by the way they have recognised his values and expressed them in their lives. Those who have responded to him have nothing to fear from God's judgement; those who have acted as if they could just make their own values and impose them on the world have everything to fear. God gave the people the responsibility for administering his earthly creation (e.g. Gen 1:28), and now they must render account.

The second angel proclaims the fall of Babylon, 'she who made all nations drink the wine of her impure passion'

(14:8). The Babylonians had captured Jerusalem and destroyed it nearly six hundred years before the birth of Christ and had taken all the leading Jews into exile. But here in the Book of Revelation, Babylon is a coded title for Rome, which had besieged and destroyed Jerusalem again only a few years before John's visions and had sold the survivors into slavery. Moreover, the Roman emperors had recently begun to declare themselves to be gods, and the cult of worshipping statues of the emperors could easily be seen as a revival of the ancient practice of making conquered peoples worship the conqueror's gods. John's flock would readily understand that 'Babylon' stood for Rome.

The third angel proclaims God's anger on all who worship the beast and its image, and who are identified by the mark of the beast branded on their foreheads. They will 'drink the wine of God's wrath' poured undiluted, and be punished eternally in the same pool of burning sulphur prepared for the devil. The language is horrific and is anticipated by such Old Testament passages as the destruction of Sodom and Gomorrah (Gen 19:24-26); the damned will have to endure their torments 'in the presence of the holy angels and in the presence of the Lamb' (14:10). In other words, they will be eternally confronted with the reason for their punishment, their rejection of the salvation made available to them by God at the cost of the crucifixion. Such imagery is difficult for the modern mind to accept, but it is pointing to the underlying theme of justice and the rejection of God's saving love.

The imagery of universal judgement and horrific punishment is continued in the next vision, of a human figure with a sickle seated on a white cloud. A voice cries out that the harvest is ripe and calls on the figure with the sickle to harvest the earth, like a reaper cutting a crop of corn. As the harvesting proceeds, an angel emerges from the temple of heaven 'and gathered the vintage of the earth, and threw it into the great wine press of the wrath of God' (14:19). John says that he saw a river of blood flow from the press and run for two hundred miles.

Much of this imagery echoes descriptions found in the Old Testament prophets. Isaiah uses the image of a winepress, such a familiar household tool in grape-growing areas, for the thoroughness of God's punishment (Is 63:3). But the most dramatic echo in these descriptions of judgement is to be found in Daniel, who spoke of a human figure enthroned on the clouds and coming to judge all nations (Dan 7:13f); at his trial Jesus claimed that this prophecy referred to himself (Mk 14:62). There can be no doubt that the human figure enthroned on the clouds in John's vision is the risen and ascended Jesus.

The seven last plagues (15:1-16:21)

In many respects the visions of the second half of the Book of Revelation mirror those of the first half, and so the seven last plagues reflect the seven plagues which seven angels released earlier with trumpet blasts (8:6-9:21).Those earlier plagues drew on the experience of persecution and helped to explain it to those who were enduring it. These plagues depict divine punishment poured out on the beast who represents the power of evil which instigated the persecutions, on all who cooperated with it, and on its earthly territory.

But first, as before, John says that he received a vision of the heavenly court from which God administers his cosmic justice on his whole creation. Prominent in the court are the faithful who had accepted persecution rather than submit to the beast and cooperate with it. They stood before God, says John, and sang the song of thanksgiving and triumph which the Hebrews had sung immediately after God had led them to freedom from their slavery in Egypt (Ex 15:1-18). That great original act of Hebrew redemption was only a foretaste of the final redemption God would enact at the end of the world.

The final, universal redemption was made possible by Jesus, Son of God, becoming human and being utterly obedient to God even to the point of crucifixion. Such obedience was a sacrifice which far surpassed all the animal sacrifices of Hebrew religion, so the faithful in the court of heaven then sang 'the song of the Lamb', celebrating Jesus, the sacrificed Lamb of God, as the revelation of God's saving justice (15:3-4).

Then the plagues begin. Seven angels process from the heavenly temple-tent and are handed seven golden bowls by one of the four great spiritual creatures always closest to God. Each bowl contains one of the seven plagues by which God would now administer his justice, and the temple is closed to all until that justice has been done.

As this series of visions is so closely related to the exodus of the ancient Hebrews from Egypt, it is not surprising that the plagues repeat many of the features of the ten plagues released on Egypt by Moses to demonstrate God's invincible power (Ex 7:14-12:34).

The first bowl of plague causes 'foul and evil sores' to break out on all people who carried the mark of the beast. The second bowl turns the sea to blood, so that every creature in it dies. In Hebrew tradition, the sea was a realm of evil and danger inhabited by Leviathan, 'the twisting serpent, ... the dragon that is in the sea' (Is 27:1) whom God would kill in the final days. The third bowl turns the rivers and springs of the earth to blood. An angel then explained the symbolism of these plagues:

> 'Just art thou in these thy judgements,
>   thou who art and wast, O Holy One.
> For men have shed the blood of saints and prophets,
>   and thou hast given them blood to drink.
> It is their due!' (16:5-6).

The plague in the fourth bowl affects the sun, which increases enormously in power and scorches all those who have blasphemed against God. Like the plagues of Egypt, neither this nor the next plague induces repentance in those who suffer from it. The fifth plague brings darkness, like the ninth plague of Egypt (Ex 10:21-23), and the sixth plague dries up the River Euphrates so that 'the kings of the East' can cross it. In the time of the early Christians when John was having his visions, these kings probably symbolised the Parthians, the main enemies on Rome's eastern frontiers who prevented the empire expanding beyond Palestine into Mesopotamia.

Three demonic spirits like frogs next appear on the scene in John's vision – again an echo of the plagues of the exodus (Ex 8:2-13) – whose task it is to call all the kings of the earth to gather for the final battle 'at the place which is called in Hebrew Armageddon' (16:16). The name literally means 'Hill of Megiddo', the site of a great Hebrew fortress guarding the coast road to the north where it crossed the ridge of Mount Carmel. The Hebrew King Josiah had been defeated there in 608 BC when he tried to withstand an Egyptian army, and the battle had changed the course of Hebrew history. Little wonder, then, that it should be the site of the final battle between God and the forces of evil.

Finally, John says that the seventh angel casts the contents of his bowl of plague into the air, and a voice from the temple-throne in heaven said, 'It is done!' There is an earthquake greater than had ever been experienced, Babylon and all the Gentile cities are destroyed, the earth is levelled and the surviving people are struck by huge hailstones. Here again there is an echo of the plagues of Egypt (Ex 9:18-33).

The seven plagues might seem to have completed the punishment and destruction of evil, but the final destruction is yet to come and meanwhile John's narrative returns to the fate of Babylon.

Babylon, the great prostitute (17:1-18)

The first Christians believed that Jesus brought about the fulfilment of all Hebrew history, so it is understandable that John's visions draw repeatedly on events in Hebrew history for their symbolic imagery. This is particularly evident in what they say about Babylon.

The Babylonians were by no means the worse conquerors the Hebrews of Palestine ever experienced, but they were the only ones before Roman times to destroy Jerusalem and its Temple. By that time, the Temple in Jerusalem had become the only place on earth where the animal sacrifices central to Hebrew religion could legally be offered. Consequently, Babylon became a particularly vivid symbol of evil for any power which threatened the Hebrew people and opposed God.

The first Christians accepted this role for Babylon along with other Hebrew symbolism, and applied it to Rome and its empire. As we have noted, the Romans destroyed Jerusalem and its Temple at the climax of the Roman-Jewish War of AD 66-70, shortly before John received his visions, thus making it inevitable that Christians would attach the Babylon symbolism to Rome.

The visions John next received serve as detailed explanations for the destruction of Babylon, and therefore as reassurances that Rome, the new Babylon persecuting John and his flock, would be singled out by God for special punishment. John says that an angel showed him Babylon in the form of a prostitute who served all the kings of the earth and intoxicated all their subjects. Rome claimed authority over the whole earth just as the great prostitute dominated and corrupted all rulers and their peoples. The city's arrogance turned into explicit blasphemy when the Roman emperors claimed to be gods who must be worshipped by all the empire's subjects. Refusal to take part in such worship became the central charge for the condemnation of Christians.

Next the angel in this vision takes John to see a woman clothed in scarlet and gold, seated on a scarlet beast with seven heads and ten horns, covered with blasphemous names. The woman holds a cup filled with the horrific and repellent signs of her obscene activities, and her name is written across her forehead, 'Babylon the great, mother of harlots and of earth's abominations (17:5). She was drunk, says

John, 'with the blood of the saints and the blood of the martyrs of Jesus' (17:5).

The angel reassures John that the beast and the prostitute are already doomed, and goes on to explain that the seven heads represent seven hills, and seven kings of which five have already fallen. The ten horns are ten more kings whose reigns will only be brief. They will make war on the Lamb of God, but he will conquer them, 'for he is Lord of Lords and King of Kings, and those with him are called and chosen and faithful' (17:14).

The allusion to Rome, with its seven hills is unmistakable, yet the language is cryptic enough for it to be safe against any charges of treason brought against Christians in a Roman court. Moreover, the seven kings refer to Roman emperors, and if the language about them were more precise it would be possible to date John's visions with confidence. The exact attributions and their significance were no doubt clear enough to John's original readers, but these original meanings have long since been lost. That, however, has not hindered subsequent generations of religious propagandists from giving precise interpretations as explanations of events in their own times.

The fall of Babylon (18:1-19:4)

Like much in John's later visions, the theme of this vision has already been anticipated in an earlier vision (14:8), but now John reports it far more extensively. This vision began, says John, with the descent from heaven of an angel of such authority and splendour that the whole earth was illuminated by it. He proclaims the fall of Babylon, destroyed by God because it had become the home of every kind of evil, had seduced the kings and peoples of the whole earth and had corrupted earth's merchants with its wealth. The list of luxuries named by the angel typifies the exotic goods which flowed into Rome from the empire's provinces and symbolised the decadence under the emperors:

'...cargo of gold, silver, jewels and pearls, fine linen, purple, silk and scarlet, all kinds of scented wood, all articles of ivory, all articles of costly wood, bronze, iron and marble, cinnamon, spice, incense, myrrh, frankincense, wine, oil, fine flour and wheat, cattle and sheep, horses and chariots, and slaves, that is, human souls. The fruit for which thy soul longed has gone from thee...' (18:12-14).

Another angel calls for God's people to leave the city before it is too late, lest they find themselves sharing in its sins and its punishment. Its destruction brings ruin on all who have profited from its insatiable desire for luxury: the merchants who traded with it, and the ship masters and sailors who carried the cargoes to it. They 'cried out as they saw the smoke of her burning, What city was like the great city? And they threw dust on their heads as they wept and mourned' (18:18f). John's vision paints a movingly detailed picture of a city which many would think was the enviable height of civilisation, but it is significant that the list of sinful luxuries reaches its climax with slavery, the traffic in human souls.

A further mighty angel appears with a rock like a great millstone and throws it into the sea as a symbol of Babylon's sudden end:

'...and the sound of harpers and minstrels,
   of flute players and trumpeters,
   shall be heard in thee no more;
and a craftsman of any craft
   shall be found in thee no more;
and the light of a lamp
   shall shine in thee no more;
and the voice of bridegroom and bride
   shall be heard in thee no more...' (18:22f).

The blood of prophets and saints have been found in her, says the angel in the vision. By the time when John was recording his visions the Christians of Rome had experienced intense persecution at least under the emperor Nero (reigned AD 54-68), and possibly from the later persecution under the emperor Domitian (AD 81-96).

The city thus condemned and destroyed by God represented both the highest achievements and the greatest decadence of civilisation. But its achievements were evil if they did not serve the worship of God and express God's values; they were corrupted by the slavery on which the city and its empire depended, and by its persecution of God's servants.

This particular vision of judgement ends with a hymn of exaltation addressed by heaven's multitudes to God, praising his judgements as true and just, and praising him for avenging the blood of his servants. As they watch the city burn they cry out, 'Allelujah! The smoke from her goes up forever and ever. And the twenty-four elders and the four living creatures fell down and worshipped God who is seated on the throne, saying, Amen. Alleluiah!' (19:3f).

The wedding of the Lamb (19:5-10)

In an extraordinary change of mood, the visions move away from punishment, plagues and destruction with all the inhabitants of heaven exalting over the pain and terror as proof of God's power and justice. The cosmic battles and condemnation to unending torture are far from over, but the next of John's visions moves to a scene of serene peace, a wedding, as if it could only be celebrated after Babylon-Rome had been destroyed.

The wedding is of the Lamb, and it is worth noticing that this is the nineteenth reference to the Lamb in the Book of Revelation; the Lamb is Jesus Christ, sacrificed to cleanse and save all who put their trust in him rather than in the earthly and diabolical powers opposed to God:

> '...the marriage of the Lamb has come,
>   and his Bride has made herself ready;
> it was granted her to be clothed with fine linen,
>   bright and pure –
> for the fine linen
>   is the righteous deeds of the saints' (19:7f).

Christ as bridegroom and the faithful as his bride is one of the most daring of all the images used in the Bible for the relationship between God and his faithful people.

The Gospels show that Jesus himself used marriage as an image to describe the relationship between himself as the Messiah and his disciples: 'Can the wedding guests mourn as long as the bridegroom is with them?' (Mt 9:15, Mk 2:19); and John the Baptist used the same imagery as the reason why Jesus had replaced him, 'I am not the Christ... He who has the bride is the bridegroom; the friend of the bridegroom... rejoices greatly at the bridegroom's voice; therefore this joy of mine is now full. He must increase, but I must decrease' (Jn 3:28-30).

Paul used the same imagery in his Letters, most notably in the long passage in his Letter to the Ephesians where he refers to Christ as the husband of the Church (Eph 5:23-32), and in his second letter to the Christians of Corinth, 'I betrothed you to Christ to present you as a pure bride to her one husband' (2 Cor 11:2). The New Testament repeatedly shows that the first Christians believed that they already enjoyed the most intimate union with the risen Christ, and therefore with God. The comparison with marriage was obvious to them, just as the Old Testament had used it for the new era of the coming Messiah.

In John's vision, the angel who was explaining his visions to him orders him to write, 'Blessed are they who have been called to the wedding feast of the Lamb' (19:9). The words recall Jesus's parable of the people invited to the wedding feast, and the kind of response they must make if they were to be worthy guests (Mt 22:3-14). Overawed by the vision, John tries to worship the angel, but he warns him not to do so because 'I am a fellow servant with you and your brethren who hold the testimony of Jesus. Worship God' (19:10). This was a further indication to John that he and his persecuted flock were equal to the angels in the sight of God.

The final battle (19:11-20:3)

The long series of visions revealing punishments and conflicts now move to their climax with John's vision of the final battle. The key figure in the vision, says John, was named 'Faithful and True' and he emerged from heaven mounted on a white horse to lead the forces of heaven mounted on white horses and clad in white.

The heavenly leader is the exalted Christ himself, as the symbols associated with him clearly indicate, and this is his 'second coming'. Although the full extent of his authority and power – his secret 'name' – is beyond the comprehension of anyone but himself (19:12), he is acclaimed as 'the Word of God', the divine title of Christ in the opening passage of John's Gospel (Jn 1:1-18). 'Word' in this context refers to the whole expression of God's will, and the commands by which he brought the cosmos into existence. Now his living 'Word' is bringing God's plans for the whole cosmos to their fulfilment.

The messianic symbols applied to Christ in this vision show that he is the instrument of God's final acts of judgement over the ultimate powers of evil. He has eyes of flame and wears many crowns; a sharp sword protruded from his mouth; he wears a robe dipped in blood and inscribed with his royal title: 'King of kings and Lord of lords' (20:16). In a phrase which echoes the great messianic prophecies of the early Isaiah, he will rule the nations with an iron sceptre (see Is 10-11).

John next saw an angel standing on the sun, who summoned all the birds to gather for God's banquet, 'to eat the flesh of kings, the flesh of captains, the flesh of mighty men, the flesh of horses and their riders, and the flesh of all men, both free and slave, both small and great' (19:18). The image evokes the scene of a great and bloody battle where the ground is littered with the dead and the sky is dark with vultures come to feed on them.

The vision develops as the beast and the kings of the earth lead their armies against Christ and the heavenly forces. The beast is thrown alive into a lake of burning sulphur, together with the 'false prophet' who had worked miracles to persuade the multitudes to follow it. The beast's leaderless army is put to the sword. The 'false prophet' is described in an earlier vision (13:11-18) where all who are deceived by it are branded with the number of the beast, 666.

Warnings about false prophets go back as far as the escape from Egypt, when Moses warned the people against being deceived by them even if they worked miracles (Deut 13:2-4); this warning is repeated by Jesus in the Gospels (Mt 24:24). Prophets must be rejected, whatever proofs they offer, if they urge people to worship other gods. In John's time, such warnings were particularly aimed at the worship of the Roman emperors.

The victory of Christ in the vision is sealed by the imprisonment of 'the dragon, that ancient serpent, who is the Devil and Satan' (20:2), who is seized by an angel holding the key of the bottomless pit. The angel chains the Devil, throws him into the pit and seals it, where the Devil is to remain for the thousand years of Christ's reign on earth.

The thousand-year reign of Christ (20:4-10)

John's next vision has captured the imagination of succeeding generations right up to the present day, even where the rest of Christian tradition has been ignored or positively rejected. It led to dramatic expectations for the year AD 1000 and at various subsequent times of crisis; Adolph Hitler alluded to it with his claims that his German republic, the Third Reich, would last for a thousand years; the idea will certainly become prominent again in some circles as AD 2000 approaches.

John says that he saw judges seated on thrones, and also the souls of people who had been beheaded for being faithful to Jesus and refusing to worship the beast. Jesus had promised his twelve disciples that they would sit with him as judges 'in the new world... judging the twelve tribes of Israel' (Mt 19:28) – where the context indicates that the twelve tribes represent the 'new' Israel, the followers of Christ. By the time of John many Christians had been beheaded by the Romans for refusing to compromise their beliefs by conforming to the state religion.

In John's vision these faithful ones come to life again to be priests of God and of Christ, and to share in Christ's reign on earth as Messiah for the next thousand years. This, says John, is the 'first resurrection', specially reserved for the martyrs, and the rest of the dead would not come to life again until the thousand years of Christ's messianic reign had ended.

At the end of the thousand years, says John, Satan will be released again and will gather earth's nations into a great army to attack 'the camp of the saints and the beloved city' (20:9). Fortunately, Satan's army will be destroyed by fire from heaven, and Satan himself thrown into the lake of burning sulphur to share in the eternal sufferings of the beast and the false prophet (see 19:20).

Some of the details of this vision are anticipated by the visions of the prophet Ezekiel (see Ezek 38-39). The general picture suggests that there are successive cycles of history – or spirals – in which the pattern of invasion, siege and battle is repeated. This indeed had been the experience of those living in Palestine throughout recorded history, but John's vision asserts that the pattern is not repeated endlessly. There will be a final phase, the messianic reign, and the cycles of violence will then be broken by the eternal triumph of God.

The Last Judgement (20:11-15)

At the end of the thousand years of messianic earthly rule, in John's vision, came the final judgement which rounded off the process of judgement and sentencing which has been implicit in all the visions. The scene, so often depicted by artists, is a cosmic courtroom, with God seated on a great white throne. John describes it in words which locate it outside the whole process of creation; earth and sky, which the Genesis account of creation depicted as a disk surmounted by a solid dome (Gen 1:6-10), disintegrate and disappear. God thus terminates all that he brought into existence at the creation of the cosmos, except the human race, as if to clear the way for the final judgement of humanity.

The dead are then seen to be standing before God's throne while books are opened which recorded all that they have done in their lives. The sea, Death and Hades yield up their dead. Death is personified here as a jailer who imprisons all who die until the time comes for their judgement, and in Hebrew tradition Hades (which is not 'hell') is the place of silence where the dead go for their shadowy existence (Ps 117:17).

As well as the books recording the lives of those being judged, a 'book of life' is produced which contains the names of all whose earthly lives have made them worthy of God's favour. Death and Hades, their power to terrify and confine humanity now ended, are consigned to the lake of fire in the vision, and any human beings whose names are not written in the book of life are thrown in after them.

Whatever else this vision may express, it asserts that each human life is created for a moral purpose, and is judged by the way that purpose has been expressed in everyday decisions and actions. It proclaims that God entrusts all human beings with a unique personal responsibility, beyond any comparable gift in the whole of the rest of the earthly creation. The opening account of creation at the beginning of the Book of Genesis has God say, 'Let us make man in our image, after our likeness... So God created man in his own image, in the image of God he created him; male and female he created them' (Gen 1:26f). God then made humanity responsible for administering the rest of the earth.

It was a breathtaking privilege, but mankind's control of

the rest of the earth had to be exercised by God's values, not by the selfish and exploitative principles which have so deeply distorted humanity's relationships with each other and with the rest of the earth and its creatures. Such an ideal of human dignity demands that God should be judge as well as creator and saviour, whatever imagery is employed to express the process of final judgement.

10

The new creation
(Rev 21:1–22:21)

The long sequence of visions recorded by John in the Book of Revelation reaches one kind of climax with the elimination of all evil from the creation, and then – as we have seen – God destroyed the universe itself. Perhaps this is the most startling moment in the whole sequence of dramatic events depicted in the book, but this elimination of the old cosmos so riddled with evil is only a clearing of the ground for God to create a new one. Before considering John's visions of the new creation it is worth pausing for a moment to consider what passed through the minds of the ancient Hebrews and the people of the New Testament when they thought about the universe. What kind of structure did they think it had?

As we can see from the opening chapter of Genesis, they thought of the earth itself as a thick disk with a solid dome covering it, surrounded on all sides by limitless water. The dome was the sky, which prevented the waters above it from flooding across the surface of the earth. The sun and moon, the other planets and the stars were suspended from the dome of the sky so that they could provide earth with light as they rotated to mark day and night and the seasons. This is what John saw destroyed by God at the end of the last judgement because God was about to replace it by a new creation: '...earth and sky fled away, and no place was found for them' (20:11). And the limitless waters surrounding the old universe were also eliminated (21:1); there was to be no trace left of the old creation.

The new heaven and the new earth (21:1-8)

The opening chapters of Genesis at the beginning of the Bible give a day-by-day description of God creating the old universe. John does not provide any account of how God brings the new heaven and earth into existence; he merely says that he saw it (21:1); then he passes straight to the purpose for which God made it. It is to be the location of a new Jerusalem:

> 'I saw the holy city, new Jerusalem, coming down out of heaven from God, prepared as a bride adorned for her husband; and I heard a great voice from the throne saying, Behold, the dwelling of God is with men. He will dwell with them, and they shall be his people, and God himself will be with them; he will wipe away every tear from their eyes, and death shall be no more, neither shall there be mourning nor crying nor pain any more, for the former things have passed away' (21:2-4).

More than anywhere else in John's visions of the apocalyptic climax of cosmic history, this vision draws attention to God's original purpose in creating the old universe, which was the world of John, his flock and their persecutors, and was also the world in which mankind had crucified the Son of God. The new world and its new Jerusalem emphasise the terrible extent of the old world's failure. God created the old creation to be one great temple, the place for everyone to worship God. That plan would have failed, except that God's only Son, Jesus the Christ, became human and worshipped God on behalf of all. This could have been the salvation of the old universe, but the contemporaries of Jesus rejected him and killed him.

The new creation is a new start, but God creates it for precisely the same purpose as the old creation: the worship of God; and the new Jerusalem is the symbol of that worship. The worship in the new Jerusalem is to be the closest possible union between God and his people, the final consequence of the life, death and resurrection of Jesus Christ. So 'the great voice from the throne' (21:3) explains to John that the city is like a bride going to meet her husband. Because the relationship between husband and wife is the closest union there can be between human beings, marriage is the nearest that human language can get to describing the final union between God and his people.

The final union with God is also described in John's vision in the language of 'covenant'. God will dwell with his people and will always be with them. So all the promises God ever made in the long series of covenants recorded in the Old Testament, and the new covenant Jesus sealed with his blood, come to their fulfilment in the new creation. The old order has passed away, but is replaced by a new order in which there is no more death, mourning, crying and pain (21:4).

This part of the vision is rounded off by God's own proclamation of his achievement, 'It is done! I am the Alpha and the Omega, the beginning and the end' (21:6). Everything that has ever happened or has ever existed comes to a focus in God, who creates and controls all things, including the human race.

But there is more to this than mere creation, as if God were only a craftsman who manufactures products which have no will of their own. Human beings are created with the freedom to respond to God, to worship him, to recognise God's values and to cooperate with him in applying his values to the rest of creation. Jesus gave the perfect demonstration of this response in his own human life on earth, and would not allow anything to stop him, even death; so he rose in glory. All who respond faithfully to God will share in such glory, 'He who conquers shall have this heritage, and I will be his God and he shall be my son' (21:7).

Those who respond to God are destined for glory, but those who reject him and his values are destined for 'the second death'. They are the cowardly, the faithless, the polluted, murderers, fornicators, sorcerers, idolaters, and all liars (21:8). The new creation is a society where there is no place for any who think that they can create their own values.

The new Jerusalem (21:9 22:5)

The new Jerusalem John describes is the ultimate temple and the fulfilment of all the covenants God ever made with mankind, the visible proof that 'the dwelling of God is with men. He will dwell with them, and they shall be his people' (21:3). For the Hebrews, the great Temple in Jerusalem used to be the visible expression of the covenant God had made with them as a nation when he rescued them from Egypt. The sacrifices offered there bridged the years and the distance which separated each successive generation from that great act of redemption. The new Jerusalem of John's vision was to be all one great temple.

The words accompanying John's vision also echo the unmistakable language of the covenant, used again and again in both the Old and the New Testament to express God's first covenant with his chosen people and then with all peoples and his whole created world. Prophets such as Jeremiah and Ezekiel had looked forward to a new covenant, in which mankind would really respond to God's love as never before (e.g. Jer 31:31-34; Ezek 36:24-30).

As his visions unfolded, John says that one of the angels who had administered the plagues carried him to a high mountain, saying, 'Come, I will show you the bride, the wife of the Lamb' (21:9). John then saw the new Jerusalem descending from heaven, radiant with the clear glory of God like a great jewel. Its high walls are pierced by twelve gates bearing the names of the twelve tribes of Israel, and the walls are built on twelve foundation stones bearing the names of the twelve apostles. Each of the stones is composed of a different kind of jewel, and each of the gates is a gigantic pearl; the streets are paved with gold so pure that it seems as transparent as glass (21:10-21).

Such a design for the city signified that the Christian Church was the new chosen people, the extension and fulfilment of the role God had originally given to the people of Israel in his plan of redemption. The twelve tribes of the new Jerusalem were no longer confined to people who could trace their descent from Abraham, but were composed of everyone who had responded to God's saving love and remained faithful to him.

There was no temple in the city because God himself and the Lamb resided in the whole city. Similarly, there was no need for a sun or a moon to provide light, because the city was illuminated by the glory of God and the Lamb. Nor was this light mere illumination; it was light to guide all peoples to God. Light is one of the most compelling symbols in the Bible for God's guidance. Old Testament prophets such as Isaiah had looked forward to the times of the Messiah when it could be said that 'the people who walked in darkness have seen a great light' (Is 9:2). God promised, they said, that he would send his servant 'as a light to the nations, that my salvation may reach to the ends of the earth' (Is 49:6).

The New Testament identifies Jesus as the promised light which 'shines in the darkness, and the darkness has not overcome it... The true light that enlightens every man' (Jn 1:5,9). John's vision of the new Jerusalem, with its rich profusion of images, presents Jesus, the Lamb of God, as a lamp from which the glory of God shines out into all the new creation:

> 'By its light shall the nations walk; and the kings of the earth shall bring their glory into it, and its gates shall never be shut by day, and there shall be no night there; they shall bring into it the glory and the honour of the nations' (21:24-26).

However dazzled John and his contemporaries may have been by the glories and luxuries of the city of Rome, the new Jerusalem is incomparably more wonderful. Moreover, the city and its inhabitants are incorrupt. In an earlier vision John had seen Rome destroyed, under the symbolic name 'Babylon', for its blasphemous arrogance; now he saw it replaced by a city worthy to be the dwelling place of God and his people. There are earlier visions in the Bible of a new Jerusalem to replace the old capital city of God's chosen people, grown corrupt by the rule of corrupt Hebrew kings and priests. The most impressive of the earlier descriptions occupies the final nine chapters of Ezekiel, and John's vision contains some of the features of Ezekiel's new city. But nothing really compares with John's description in which the language points beyond what can be imagined, towards the indescribable glory of God.

'The river of the water of life' flows from the throne of God in John's vision, and on through the city. As in the Garden of Eden (Gen 2:9), the tree of life grows by the river, with fruit for each month and leaves which heal all wounds and sicknesses. The tree of life in the story of Eden conferred immortality, and God had driven mankind away from it because they had turned away from God to create their own values (Gen 3:22-24); God could not permit the resulting confusion to be perpetuated by undying generations. In the new Jerusalem the tree of life grows in profusion and is available to all.

Now, at this climax of John's visions, the whole of humanity is living by the light of God and is worshipping him as he shares the glory of the new Jerusalem with them. There is no reason now for God to deny them immortality, so they all have unhindered access to the fruit of the tree of life. With a symmetry which binds the whole Christian Bible into a unity, the final chapter of John's visions returns to one of the most vivid incidents at the beginning of Genesis. In the new creation mankind is given the ultimate gift of immortality which God had originally wished it to have from the very beginning of the old creation.

Epilogue (22:6-21)

The Book of Revelation ends with a number of strong assertions that the information it contains is true. Most of the epilogue is occupied by words spoken to John by Jesus himself, beginning with the reassurance from Jesus that 'these words are trustworthy and true' (22:6).

John was conducted through his long series of visions by an angel who, says Jesus, was sent by God to reveal what must soon take place. The decisive proof of truth, however, will be the return of Jesus to earth, 'And behold, I am coming soon' (22:7). Within the context of eternity 'soon' can seem to be a very long time, but the words imply that the second coming of Jesus in judgement will be the irrefutable confirmation of all that John had seen.

John then says that he, the author of the book, is the one who actually heard and saw what he has recorded in it. He repeats the scene where he tried to worship the angel who was guiding him, and the angel told him that he was only a fellow servant with John, with prophets like John and with all who respond to the warnings in the book (22:8f; see 19:10).

John returns to reporting what Jesus was saying to him. John was told not to seal up his book to await future generations. Time has run out, the words imply, and there is no longer any point in concealing the revelations in the hope that humanity will change its ways. Jesus says that he is coming soon 'to repay everyone for what he has done' (22:12).

Jesus adds that he is 'the Alpha and the Omega', the titles designating total existence which God had applied to himself a little earlier in the vision of the new Jerusalem (21:6), 'the first and the last, the beginning and the end' (22:13). The opening words of John's Gospel say that Jesus the Christ was present at the beginning of the universe as God's divine agent of creation; he is also the divine agent of fulfilment and judgement at the end of the old creation and the formation of the new order.

The message of the visions is summarized: those who 'wash their robes' may enter the new Jerusalem; all others will be excluded (7:14f). The washing of robes refers back to one of the first visions when John saw a great crowd of people in white robes who had 'washed their robes and made them white in the blood of the Lamb' (7:14). Washing anything in blood could easily seem a savage idea, but it would be a mistake to think that John is using a crude image here. Hebrews believed that the blood of the sacrifices offered in the Temple was filled with God's power to cleanse from ritual sins. Christianity continues this belief but applies it to Christ's death; the blood of Christ's crucifixion, the ultimate sacrifice, cleanses worshippers from all sin if only they put their entire trust in it.

Jesus again reminds John of the reason why he has been chosen to receive such revelations; it is so that John can make them known to the Churches. That is how the Book of Revelation begins: 'The revelation of Jesus Christ, which God gave him to show to his servants...' (1:1), and this explanation for all the visions is now repeated at the end of the book. Then Jesus says, 'I am the root and the offspring of David, the bright morning star' (22:16). Early in the book Jesus had told John that he would 'give the morning star' to whoever 'conquers and keeps my works to the end' (2:26-28). The morning star is the sign that the new day is near, and Jesus is the sign that the new creation is near, the 'Son of David' of the old messianic hopes who will make all God's promises come true (e.g. Is 9:6f).

John now moves to his own words, to begin to carry out the responsibility Jesus has laid on him. John delivers three impassioned invitations for all to come and accept the offer of life which God so freely holds out to them:

> 'The Spirit and the Bride say, Come. And let him who hears say, Come. And let him who is thirsty come, let him who desires take the water of life without price' (22:17).

The invitation is first offered by the Spirit and the Bride, the community of those who have already accepted Jesus Christ as their saviour; it is repeated by those who hear the invitation and respond to it; and it is open to all who realise that they want the salvation that God offers. But it remains an invitation which can be refused. Love looks for a free response, else it is not love, not even God's love, especially not God's love.

John passes on to warnings. The revelations he has recorded have to be accepted in their entirety and without additions. It is an apt warning, for revelation is a powerful force. There have always been those who want to use God's revelation to increase their own power over others, but they can only do so if they select from it, expand it and distort it to fit their own interpretations of it. The fullness of God's revelation exposes all attempts to distort it and use it for lesser ends than the ones that God intends.

Apart from the final words of blessing, the book ends with Jesus' own assurance, 'Surely I am coming soon' (22:20), and John's fervent personal response, 'Amen. Come, Lord Jesus!' (22:20).

This immensely complex book of ecstatic visions will only make full sense to those who can say in all honesty that this final prayer of John's is their own also.

Conclusion

More than anywhere else in the whole Bible, even more than in the opening chapters of the Book of Genesis or in God's commands to the invading Hebrews that they must exterminate the Canaanites, the New Testament language about the end of the universe challenges us to ask what kind of teaching this is.

One kind of answer is easy to give: many Christians just say that all of it is literally true and that this is exactly how the universe will end. They usually take this view because some of the other statements in the New Testament are so important that they have to take them literally or lose all faith in Jesus Christ as their Saviour. If they question the literal accuracy of the New Testament's descriptions of the Last Judgement, how can they accept the truth of Jesus' resurrection from the dead? Or believe that Jesus really told Peter that he was the Rock on which the Church was to be built?

This is sometimes called 'fundamentalism'. Down the centuries this attitude towards the Bible has caused people to do such appalling things to each other in the name of God that this approach must be treated with caution. We cannot just suspend reason and swallow the Bible whole without at least questioning the vivid imagery in it.

The beginnings of an answer can be found in the experience Paul describes in the Second Letter to the Corinthians. He was angry when he wrote it because the Christians of Corinth had been misled by other teachers and Paul was dismayed by their rejection of what he himself had taught them. He wrote to them reluctantly about ecstatic visions of heaven he himself had experienced:

'I knew a man in Christ (he is referring to himself) who fourteen years ago was caught up to the third heaven – whether in the body or out of the body I do not know, God knows. And I know that this man was caught up into Paradise – whether in the body or out of the body I do not know, God knows – and he heard things that cannot be told, which man may not utter' (2 Cor 12:2-4).

Paul is telling his beloved friends in Corinth that there are truths beyond words, truths which words in their inadequacy can easily betray. He had said as much to them in an earlier letter, as we have seen, about the resurrection of the body. 'What kind of body will it be?' they had asked him, and Paul's answer showed that words could not describe it (1 Cor 15:35-58). As we penetrate further into the heart of such mysteries we come nearer to silence; not the silence of ignorance but the silence of a knowledge far too great to be expressed by any human images.

The limitations of language confronted by the mystery of God has been recognised by all the great religions, and it is embedded deeply in the history of Christianity itself. The fifth century Christian writings attributed – wrongly – to the Dionysius of Acts 17:34 still challenge theologians to reflect on what they think they are doing when they make statements about God. One of the shortest works in that early collection, 'The Mystical Theology', ends with an uncompromising assertion that it is not possible to speak accurately about God at all, because 'the supreme cause of every conceptual being is not itself conceptual':

'There is no speaking of it, nor name nor knowledge of it. Darkness and light, error and truth – it is none of these. It is beyond assertion and denial. We make assertions and denials of what is next to it, but never of it, for it is beyond every assertion, being the unique cause of all things, and, by virtue of its pre-eminently simple and absolute nature, free of every limitation' ('The Mystical

Theology', 5, trans. C Luibheid, in *Pseudo-Dionysius*, London: SPCK, 1987).

Language sets limits to what it is describing. God is beyond all limitations of even the most powerful human imagination.

If this is the case, every assertion about the relationship between mankind and God is potentially false and misleading, including every word of the Bible. A growing sense of this inadequacy may be detected in the works of the Hebrew prophets. The earlier prophets, such as Amos and Hosea, made firm, clear assertions about God as judge or as husband; Isaiah's vision of God enthroned in the Temple is clear and precise (Is 6:1-4). But by the time of the exile of the Hebrew people in Babylonia, Ezekiel clearly felt that the words he used were woefully inadequate to express the experience of being in God's presence:

> 'Over the heads of the living creatures was what looked like a solid surface glittering like crystal... When they moved it was like the noise of flood waters, like the voice of Shaddai, like the noise of a storm, like the noise of an armed camp... Beyond the solid surface above their heads, there was what seemed like a sapphire, in the form of a throne. High above on the form of a throne was a form with the appearance of a human being (Ez 1:22,24,26).

At the end of the exile the Second Isaiah proclaimed the unequalled power of God to save, but:

> 'To whom can you compare me, or who is my equal? says the Holy One... Yahweh is the everlasting God, he created the remotest parts of the earth. He does not grow tired or weary, his understanding is beyond fathoming... Let the wicked abandon his way and the evil one his thoughts. Let him turn back to Yahweh who will take pity on him, to our God, for he is rich in forgiveness; for

my thoughts are not your thoughts and your ways are not my ways, declares Yahweh' (Is 40:25,28; 55:7-8).

The impossibility of any human understanding of God was forced on the prophets by their growing discovery that God's forgiveness is quite irrational by human standards of justice. Later still, in works such as Job and Qoheleth (Ecclesiastes), the Old Testament said that those who attempt to speak adequately and accurately about God find that their efforts drive them into silence.

The New Testament represents a radically different belief about the form that the divine revelation takes. God now reveals himself uniquely in a human being – Jesus – rather than in laws or in verbal revelations of his will. Assertions about God can now take a new form; they can escape from the restrictions of decrees whose words have absolute authority which must be obeyed to the letter.

Jesus himself is the expression of God's will; his own life is the standard for response to God's will; and he is also the new covenant, the means by which such a response becomes possible: 'This is my blood, which seals God's covenant, my blood poured out for many for the forgiveness of sins' (Mt 26:28), where 'blood' – in accordance with Jewish beliefs – is the symbol of life, and sacrificial blood is the means of sharing in God's life.

So Paul could write of Jesus as the perfect mediator of God's promises and of mankind's response to them: 'For in him is found the Yes to all God's promises and therefore it is through him that we answer Amen to give praise to God' (2 Cor 1:20). Faith-commitment to Jesus, who is both human and divine, both dead and risen in glory, becomes one of the central themes of the New Testament and replaces the Old Testament emphasis on obedience to law.

When Jesus taught, he used a complex of analogies drawn from everyday life, but he controlled the conclusions he wanted his listeners to draw from them. This is most clearly seen in the parables which use the analogy of a kingdom, the form of political structure most familiar to his Jewish audience. But Jesus makes it clear that his use of 'kingdom' differs from the secular model: it comes into existence by a different process – more like a plant growing from a seed; people cannot inherit membership from their parents by being 'sons of Abraham', membership is by invitation of the king.

Jesus himself is the king, but his kingdom is not of this world – so there will be no visible, theocratic state; yet his kingdom is intended to come on earth, as in heaven; some of the members of this kingdom are harmful to it, like weeds growing in wheat, but the other members must not try to weed them out; the kingdom of heaven works mysteriously and secretly in the world, like yeast working in bread until everything is transformed by it. Jesus' listeners have to draw their own conclusions, but they must follow him and accept his point of view to reach the right conclusions.

Jesus' language becomes far more explicit when he told his disciples what would happen at the end of the world. He spoke to them of terrible wars, Jerusalem in ruins, terror reigning and cosmic disasters. Both he and they were living within a particular religious tradition, Judaism, and he was using images familiar to them all.

Similarly, Jesus and his contemporaries in Palestine had inherited images which they could use as symbols of hope in God's salvation and triumph over evil: the faithful shepherd; the king who won peace and freedom for his people; the secure city and refuge; the temple where God could be found; the healing and purifying rites of sacrifice; the earthly paradise of a land flowing with milk and honey; the harmony of mankind with all the rest of creation; the divine law revealed as a practical guide for a perfect human society; a covenant of eternal loyalty between God and man.

When the symbols confuse us or repel us, we only have to turn back to Jesus himself and what happened to him, for this is the only certain truth about the future, even if it cannot be put accurately into words. We know that he was conceived and born a fully human being like us. We know that he lived and coped with the endless surprises of human life like us. We know that he died like us, though we would wish to be spared the kind of death he died.

Once we begin to realise that all that part of Jesus' existence – from his birth to his death – is true to our own experience, we can begin to tackle the rest of what the New Testament tells about him: that he already existed before the whole cosmos was made; that he was raised by God from the dead and ascended – human and divine – to God again; that he now rules as Lord of the universe; that he will be at the centre of events as Judge and Saviour when God ends the present cosmos and brings a new creation into being.

All this matters to us because we are part of it. We shall all die, but we are told that we can share in Jesus' passage through death to the risen life of full communion with God. God intends that we should be children of God as fully as Jesus is Son of God, 'heirs of God and fellow heirs with Christ', as Paul puts it, and that the whole creation is somehow caught up in this fellowship of glory (Rom 8:16-23).

Time past, time present and time future all coalesce in what God has revealed to us through his Son and in what his Son has done for us. Our end came at the crucifixion of Jesus, when the forces of destruction reached their climax in their assault on his life, and he was nailed bodily to the cross and died; but the blood he shed there was the ultimate life force, and in shedding it he made it available for us to share.

The very heart of the Christian tradition tells us that we are already united with him, both in his death and in his life beyond death; so the life we now live is the life of the risen Jesus, body and blood; we are living in the end itself. And when the end comes in all its decisive finality, it will come to us in the person of the Jesus who died, who now shares his risen life with us, and who has promised to bring us to the ultimate consummation for which we and all the cosmos have been made.

So why do we feel such fear about our end? It is because we know that love enters into it, and we also know full well that the love we offer in response to God's love is pathetically inadequate. We are indeed lost if we have to love God to the same extent that God loves us.

Yet there is no good cause for worry, for God has already met our problem by his gift of the Holy Spirit to us:

> 'All who are led by the Spirit of God are sons of God. For you did not receive the spirit of slavery to fall back into fear, but you have received the spirit of sonship. When we cry, Abba! Father! it is the spirit himself bearing witness with our spirit that we are children of God' (Rom 8:14-16).

By his Spirit, God amplifies our love for God so that it can match his love for us; then we truly become his children with all the security that goes with this. We have the reassurance of Jesus himself about God's ultimate intentions for us at the final times: 'Fear not, little flock, for it is your Father's pleasure to give you the kingdom' (Lk 12:32).

Suggestions for further reading

All the biblical quotations in this book are taken, with permission, from the *Revised Standard Version* (RSV) of the Bible. This is a good translation, widely approved by most Christian Churches, including the Roman Catholic Church. Some other modern translations are easier to use because they divide the material into paragraphs and sections with headings. These include *The New Jerusalem Bible* and *The Good News Bible*.

J. Rhymer, *The Bible in Order* (1975), presents all the contents of the Bible in a chronological order to show how the various strands of teaching developed, and how they relate to the events of the times.

There are a number of general *commentaries* on the Bible, which have good sections on the themes of this book, either under individual books of the Bible, or under such headings as 'apocalyptic', 'eschatology' and 'messiah'. These include:

New Bible Commentary, edited by G. Guthrie and others (3rd edition, 1970)
The New Jerome Biblical Commentary, edited by R.E. Brown and others (1989)

There are numerous books on Jesus and the *Gospels*, which comment on his teaching, including the 'final times'. Some of these are:

R. Cantalamessa, *Jesus Christ the Holy One of God* (1991)

H. Conzelmann, *Jesus* (1973)
M. Cook, *The Jesus of Faith* (1981)
C.H. Dodd, *The Apostolic Preaching and its Developments* (1936)
C.H. Dodd, *The Founder of Christianity* (1971)
L. Goppelt, *The Theology of the New Testament* (1981)
A.M. Hunter, *The Work and Words of Jesus* (1950)
J. Mackey, *Jesus the Man and the Myth* (1979)
N. Perrin, *Rediscovering the Teaching of Jesus* (1967)
V. Taylor, *The Gospels* (1960)
G. Vermes, *Jesus the Jew* (1973)
D. Watson, *Jesus Then and Now* (1983)
I. Wilson, *Jesus: the Evidence* (1984).

There are many books specifically on the themes of the 'final times'. The following is a small selection from them:

A. Farrer, *The Revelation of St John the Divine* (1964)
W.J. Harrington, *The Apocalypse of St John* (1969)
P.E. Hughes, *The Book of Revelation* (1990)
O. Lewry, *The Theology of History* (1969)
M. Simpson, *Death and Eternal Life* (1970)
C. McDannell and B. Lang, *Heaven, a History* (1988)
S. Mowinckel, *He That Cometh* (1959)
D.S. Russell, *The Method and Message of Jewish Apocalyptic* (1964)
D. Tiede, *Jesus and the Future* (1990)
R. Van der Hart, *The Theology of Angels* (1971)

General Index

Abraham: 30
Adam: 11, 30, 71, 105
Angels: 60, 65, 86, 93f, 98f, 119, 124
Antichrist: 45, 113
Apocalyptic discourses of Jesus: 44f
Apostolic Beliefs: 16f
Armageddon: 121
Augustine of Hippo: 66f

Babylon, Babylonia: 30, 117f, 122f
Baptism: 17, 18, 56, 61f, 75, 89
Benedictus: 28
Bethlehem: 26f
Blood: 67f, 83, 89f, 118, 139, 146

Church: 18, 19, 34, 51, 68, 79, 93, 110, 136f
Community: 18, 55f, 69
Covenant: 14, 26, 27, 30, 48, 67, 83, 105, 135
Creation Stories: 11ff, 95f, 98, 105f, 130f, 133f
Creation: 11, 23, 26, 56, 82, 95, 115, 117, 133f

David: 14, 30, 44, 75, 83
Day of the Lord: 26, 38
Devil: *see* Satan
Dies Irae: 8
Dürer: 19

Eden: 71
Elders: 81
Elijah: 31
Emmanuel: 31
Escatology: 10, 21, 43, 51
Eucharist: 18, 38, 46ff, 56, 89, 146
Eve: 11, 71, 105
Exodus from Egypt: 14, 25f, 73, 83, 95, 98, 119f

Fall: 11, 105
False Messiahs: 45
Fertility religions: 71, 74, 75, 117
Flood: 11f

Gentile Christians: 57f
Good Shepherd: 14
Gospels: 15ff, 21ff
Greeks: 45, 71

History: 22, 23, 81, 84, 101, 103, 121f
Holy Spirit: 16, 22, 26, 28f, 34, 49, 52, 56, 63, 140, 149
Horsemen of the Apocalypse: 85f
Hymns: 7, 17, 81

Israel, Tribes of: 86f, 105

Jerusalem (and New J.): 14f, 26f, 60, 71, 76, 80, 134f
Jesus, Ascension: 16, 27, 47f, 51, 101, 119
 Birth: 16
 Death: 16, 24, 27, 35ff, 47, 76, 119
 Hour of: 39f
 Infancy: 30
 Incarnation: 16, 24, 105
 Judge: 16, 25, 40, 74, 76, 83f, 91
 Lamb of God: 83, 86, 115, 116, 125f
 Lord of the Universe: 17, 51, 63, 68, 101, 105, 123, 148
 Messiah: 13ff, 30, 33, 35, 40, 42
 Resurrection: 16, 25, 27, 35ff, 47, 76, 119
 Sacrifice: 89f
 Second Coming: 16, 19, 51, 56, 63, 139
 Son of God: 74, 119

Son of Man: 45f, 68, 111
Temptations: 61
Word of Creation: 23ff, 42, 127
John the Baptist: 28, 31, 83
John's Gospel: 23ff, 43
Journey in Luke: 27
Judgement: 14, 16, 19, 21, 24, 46, 70, 83, 84ff, 93f
Kingdom of God: 19, 21f, 32f, 146f

Lamb (diabolical): 111, 113
Language and imagery: 64ff, 90, 91, 143ff
Last Judgement (*see also* Judgement) 60, 129f
Last Supper: *see* Eucharist
Law: 13, 24, 57f
Letters of N.T.: 17f, 51ff
Luke: 25ff, 30, 43, 51

Maccabean Wars: 45
Manna: 73
Mark: 43
Mary: 27, 28, 30, 39, 105f
Matthew: 30, 32
Messiah: 13f, 22, 25, 43ff, 75, 105
Messianic Age, Kingdom: 14, 21, 28f, 32, 52, 56, 63
Messianic Battle: 43, 108f, 127f
Michael: 108f
Michelangelo: 19
Millennium: 128
Miracles: 36ff
Monotheism: 11
Moses: 67, 128
Mount of Olives: 43, 46

Name: 73

Nazareth: 26, 28
Nero: 113, 125
New Covenant: 24, 59, 63, 100
New Creation: 24f, 30, 133ff
New Testament Chronology: 52ff
Number symbolism: 66, 94, 112f
Nunc Dimittis: 28

Parables: 31ff, 44, 46
Parthians: 121
Passover: 43, 46ff, 83
Patmos: 69
Paul: 17f, 29, 54ff, 70, 110
Pentecost: 29, 52
Persian Empire: 112
Prophets: 14, 23, 99, 119, 145
Psalms: 59, 90

Resurrection: 56
Revelation, Book of: chapters 5-10, 65ff
River of Life: 138
Rome: 26, 52, 72, 75, 112, 118, 122f

Sacrifices: 59f, 67f, 83, 86, 117, 139
Satan: 72, 108f, 128f
Second Coming: *see* Jesus
Solomon: 14
Suffering: 14, 69, 72, 84, 88f, 100

Temple: 27, 30, 40, 43, 44, 47, 59, 80, 99f, 101, 122, 136f
Time: 67, 115, 148
Tree of Knowledge, 105
Tree of Life: 71, 138

Underworld: 97

Index of Biblical references

Genesis:
- 1-11 — p 11
- 1 — p 23
- 1:2 — p 26
- 1:6-10 — p 130
- 1:26f — p 130
- 1:28 — p 117
- 2:9 — p 71, 138
- 2:14 — p 98
- 3 — p 105f
- 3:1-6 — p 108
- 3:22-24 — p 71, 138
- 19:24-26 — p 118
- 49:9 — p 83

Exodus:
- 3 — p 67
- 7:14–12:34 — p 120
- 7:17-21 — p 95
- 8:2-13 — p 121
- 9:18-33 — p 121
- 9:22-26 — p 95
- 10:3-20 — p 98
- 10:21-23 — p 121
- 12-14 — p 43, 83
- 14:19-24 — p 14
- 15:1-18 — p 119
- 16:15-36 — p 73
- 19:6 — p 67, 84, 100
- 24:3-8 — p 48

Numbers:
- 22–24 — p 73

Deuteronomy:
- 13:2-4 — p 128
- 29:18 — p 96
- 30:11-14 — p 24

Judges:
- 18 — p 87

1 Samuel:
- 28:8-19 — p 97

2 Samuel:
- 7 — p 75

1 Kings:
- 12:28-30 — p 87
- 18–21 — p 74

1 Chronicles:
- 21:1 — p 108

Job:
- 1–2 — p 108

Psalm:
- 23 — p 90
- 117:17 — p 130
- 118:26 — p 44
- 147:15,18f — p 23

Isaiah:
- 6 — p 80
- 6:2f — p 81, 145
- 7:14 — p 31
- 9:2 — p 137
- 9:6f — p 24, 140
- 10–11 — p 127
- 10:20-22 — p 87
- 22:22 — p 75
- 27:1 — p 120
- 40:25,28 — p 146
- 40:31 — p 109
- 49:6 — p 137
- 54:5-8 — p 107
- 55:7-8 — p 146
- 56:7 — p 44
- 63:3 — p 119

Jeremiah:
- 7:11 — p 44
- 31:31-35 — p 24, 59, 136

Ezekiel:
- 1,10 — p 80, 145
- 1:5ff — p 81
- 2:8–3:3 — p 99
- 9:15-16 — p 96

36:24-30	p 136		13:3-37	p 21, 44
37	p 24		14:62	p 68, 119
38–39	p 129		15:61	p 48
Daniel:			Luke:	p 31
7–8	p 46, 48, 68, 107, 119		1:32f	p 30
			1:35	p 28
9:27	p 45		2:49	p 27
10:5-19	p 69		3:22	p 28
12:6-13	p 99		3:23-38	p 30
			4:2,10	p 108
Joel:			4:18f	p 22
2:28-31	p 26		9:51	p 27
Obadiah:			12:32	p 149
17	p 116		21:7-36	p 21, 44
Zechariah:			22:15-18	p 47
9:9	p 43		22:19-20	p 47
Malachi:			John:	
4:1-3	p 38f		1:1-13	p 25, 127
4:6	p 31		1:29	p 83, 113
1 Maccabees:			2:4	p 40
1:54	p 45		3:28-30	p 126
Matthew:			4:21-23	p 40
1:1-17	p 30		5:25	p 40
5:3-10	p 22, 66		6:49-58	p 73
9:15	p 126		7:30	p 40f
12:26	p 108		8:20	p 41
16:18	p 97		12:23-27	p 41
16:23	p 108		12:31f	p 25
18:20	p 70		12:35f	p 25
19:28	p 129		13:1	p 41
21:5	p 43		13:2,27	p 109
21:9	p 43		16:21	p 42
21:28–22:14	p 44		16:32	p 42
22:3-14	p 126		17:1-5	p 42
23:1-39	p 44		19:30	p 24
24:3-24	p 21		Acts:	
24:30f	p 46		1:6	p 51
24:3-51	p 44		1:10f	p 52
24:15	p 45		2:33	p 28
24:24	p 112, 128		9:1-19	p 55
25:45f	p 46		15:1-34	p 58, 72
26:27-28	p 89, 146		17:35	p 144
26:29	p 47		20:29-30	p 71
Mark:			22:6-16	p 55
1:13	p 108		26:12-18	p 55
1:15	p 22		Romans:	
2:19	p 126		3:21-26	p 57
11.10	p 44		6:3-11	p 55
11:17	p 44		8:14-16	p 149

8:16-23	p 77, 148
10:9	p 17
12:4-10	p 55
12:13	p 88
1 Corinthians:	
12:12-30	p 55
10:16	p 57
11:17-34	p 63
11:26	p 57
15:35-57	p 56, 144
2 Corinthians	
1:3-7	p 69
1:20	p 146
11:2	p 126
11:12-15	p 112
12:2-4	p 144
Galatians:	
2:11-14	p 58
3:27	p 89
Ephesians:	
1:3-14	p 56
5:23-32	p 126
Philippians:	
2:4	p 101
3:20f	p 56
Colossians:	
1:15-20	p 18
1 Thessalonians:	
4:16f	p 57
Hebrews:	
1:3f	p 58
7:26f	p 59
9:28	p 60
10:26-31	p 60
12:22-24	p 60
12:28f	p 60
James:	
5:8	p 63
1 Peter:	
1:6f	p 61
2:9	p 100
3:21	p 62
4:7	p 62
1 John:	
4:16-18	p 10
Revelation:	
1:1–3:22	pp 65ff
4:1–8:1	pp 79ff
8:2–11:19	pp 93ff
12:1–13:18	pp 105ff
14:1–20:15	pp 115ff
21:1–22:21	pp 133ff

THE MIRACLES OF JESUS

Joseph Rhymer

The gospel accounts of the miracles Jesus did are sometimes dismissed as exaggerations by Christian propagandists or as naive explanations of unusual phenomena by people living in a primitive age.

But this study shows that the best way to understand the miracles of Jesus is to see them as an integral part of the pattern of early Christian beliefs. The miracles Jesus worked were offered along with other evidence to prove the divine authority of Jesus' teaching.

However, the first Christians did not blindly accept such reports. They tested and verified these data through independent testimonies. That process of verification is resumed in *The Miracles of Jesus*. The book looks at the questions we can ask today about Jesus miracles. Each miracle is then studied in detail against the general structure which supports the teaching of Jesus.

We all live by patterns of beliefs even if we are not aware of them. This may also be true in the case of what we believe about Jesus. And this book makes us realise that Jesus was not a mere worker of miracles. It renews our faith in him as the Son of God, the sign of God's love for us, and the salvation of the world.

ISBN 0 85439 387 0   £5.95